F0112 14

Can She Bake a Cherry Pie?

Can She Bake a Cherry Pie?

AMERICAN WOMEN AND THE KITCHEN
IN THE TWENTIETH CENTURY

Mary Drake McFeely

UNIVERSITY OF MASSACHUSETTS PRESS   AMHERST

Printed in the United States of America

LC 00-023452
ISBN 1-55849-250-X

Designed by Sally Nichols
Set in Janson Text by Graphic Composition, Inc.
Printed and bound by Sheridan Books, Inc.

This book is published with the support and cooperation of the University of
Massachusetts Boston.

Library of Congress Cataloging-in-Publication Data

McFeely, Mary Drake.
    Can she bake a cherry pie? : American women and the kitchen in the twentieth
century / Mary Drake McFeely.
        p. cm.
    Includes bibliographical references and index.
    ISBN 1-55849-250-X (cloth : alk. paper)
        1. Women cooks—United States—History—20th century. 2. Cookery,
American—History—20th century. I. Title.

TX649.A1 M38 2000
641.5973'082—dc21
                                                                    00-023452
                                                                         CIP

British Library Cataloguing in Publication data are available.

Chapter 5, "The War in the Kitchen," appeared in an earlier version in *Produce &
Conserve, Share & Play Square: The Grocer & the Consumer on the Home-Front Battlefield
during World War II*, ed. Barbara McLean Ward (Portsmouth, N.H.: Strawbery
Banke Museum, 1994).

For Bill

Contents

Acknowledgments

I AM VERY GRATEFUL FOR TWO FELLOWSHIPS THAT PROVIDED
TIME, RESOURCES, AND STIMULATING COLLEAGUES WHILE I WAS
working on this book. A fellowship at the Schlesinger Library, Radcliffe College, allowed me a year of immersion in its cookbook collection, a marvelous resource, at the very beginning of my research.
Barbara Haber, curator of printed books, gave me much-needed support and advice then and has continued to do so since. The staff of
the Schlesinger provided access to resources, comfortable working
conditions, and a cheerful spirit. The collegial sharing of ideas among
scholars is a tremendous asset to the solitary researcher.

As a fellow at the Rockefeller Foundation's Bellagio Study and
Conference Center in Italy, I experienced an atmosphere in which it
is impossible not to thrive. There, both solitude and companionship
are supplied in good measure.

Thomas G. Dyer loaned me his treasured copy of *The Napton
Memorial Church Cook Book* and shared his personal recollections of
life in Missouri. Charlotte Ann Metzger shared information about her
family, especially her mother and aunt, Virginia and Mary Abney. Barbara McLean Ward and the staff of the Strawbery Banke Museum
in Portsmouth, New Hampshire, led me to Louise Grant's diary. My
participation in a conference there on the home front in World War
II helped shape my ideas on wartime cooking. Access to the Julia
Child Papers at the Schlesinger Library greatly enhanced my understanding of Child's influence.

Many people have talked with me about cooking; everyone has at least one story and all helped develop my picture of twentieth century cooking. I appreciate especially my conversations with June Ball, Anna Hamburger, Joan McPherson, Ludlow Smethurst, and Dorothy Sterling. Along the way, others have added interesting insights based on their own kitchen experiences.

I am happy to join the many people to whom Linda Kerber has served as mentor. From the time this idea first came to me, through the whole process of turning it into a book, right up to the last revision, she has listened, discussed, encouraged, read, and generally supported this venture.

Carol Houck-Smith and Angela von der Lippe helped me greatly with sensitive readings. To my great benefit, Eliza McFeely and I have shared many a conversation about cultural history and the consumer society. I am indebted also to an anonymous reader whose astute comments aided a final revision. My editor, Paul Wright, supplied enthusiastic support when I most needed it. Pam Wilkinson helped greatly with her scrupulous and perceptive copyediting.

William S. McFeely knows this text almost as well as I do. His patience in reading draft after draft and his gentle but determined urging were indispensable.

M. D. M.

Can She Bake a Cherry Pie?

Women's Work

TALENT IN THE KITCHEN HAS LONG BEEN CONSIDERED AN
IMPORTANT QUALITY IN A WOMAN, AND THE QUESTION, "BUT
can she cook?" has been a symbolic way not only of rating her domestic ability but also of putting her in her female "place." In the old
American folk song "Billy Boy," a young man and his mother have a
dialogue about the woman he wants to marry. "She's the joy of my
life," he raves, describing her dimple and her ringlets, but his mother
demands, "Can she bake a cherry pie?" Beauty, charm, and intelligence in a wife were very fine, but a good cook was a treasure. In the
rural America of the past, a woman's reputation might be attached to
her cherry pie—or her chocolate layer cake, or, in the South, her biscuits. As the world changed and women entered the labor force in
increasing numbers and battled their way to success in the professions, cooking remained as a sign that a woman took her gendered
responsibilities seriously.

As "women's work," cooking has been used—and resisted—as a
tool of repression. The woman who has to provide a hot dinner for
her husband and family every night is effectively tethered to the stove
and limited in how much she can accomplish in the outside world.
Fulfilling her obligations to husband and family inhibits her ability to
act in public. At the same time, cooking has been an area of work that
women controlled, often when they controlled little else.

The irony of American women's relationship to the kitchen over
the course of the twentieth century is that as home cooking became

I

less essential, indeed more and more an option, it continued to be perceived not only by society but often by women themselves as a measure of a woman's true value.

In the nineteenth century, well-off Americans were quite content to have servants do the actual work of marketing and cooking. Finding and training a good cook was a subject of much anxious discussion, but the woman of the house was more likely to supervise than to work in the kitchen. In the twentieth century, technology began to alleviate the hard physical labor in the kitchen and even showed potential for eliminating the need to cook for an individual household at all. But if economic forces (in the shape of opportunities to work in factories, offices, and stores) drew domestic servants away from middle-class families, a moral imperative seemed to surround the obligation of the woman of the house to prepare dinner and breakfast—and sometimes lunch—herself. New, less arduous, but still time-consuming tasks accompanied the new labor-saving appliances, and new reasons were found for keeping women in the kitchen.

During the twentieth century, more and more household tasks were farmed out—to the local laundry, to the manufacturer of clothing, to the pharmacy where over-the-counter medications took the place of remedies once devised in the kitchen. But of all the activities that go into maintaining a family, cooking and child-rearing have been the most resistant to the trend. Although child rearing, with both parents working or one parent managing alone, presents society with the major problem of raising the next generation, cooking does not carry so obvious a burden. And yet food has such symbolic value that when the subject is home cooking, confused feelings abound. Over the decades of the twentieth century, cooking, the value of which had once needed no explanation, acquired various new raisons d'être, demanding of women (whose traditional responsibility for this part of life did not fade) more complex knowledge, not only of cooking techniques but of the science of nutrition, the business of consumerism, and the uneasy art of creating a happy family.

Women are consumers of images as well as goods. As fashion magazines sell body images, cookbooks sell images of the cook as scientist, artist, master chef, efficiency expert, perfecter of domestic bliss, earth protector, or patriot. In the face of a dwindling necessity for hard work in the kitchen, these images have encouraged consumerism and persuaded women to stay in the kitchen by proposing fantasy roles intended to make cooking provide some of the satisfaction we expect of paid work.

But by the end of the century, the middle-class woman was likely to be employed and finding this satisfaction—or trying to find it—in her profession. Increasingly, work, the public life, seemed to be "real life." Restaurant and take-out food replaced home cooking, and the family dinner might yield to conflicting individual schedules. For those who enjoyed it, cooking at home became almost a secret pleasure: the escape, the recreation, the absorbing, sometimes challenging activity in which the cook sometimes achieves a triumph. The triumph is brief—the achievement was, after all, made to be consumed—but failures are equally short-lived.

Cookbooks have acted as agents of society, delivering expectations of women that may conflict with or support women's own goals. We still think of domestic cooking as gendered, as female, even while more and more men voluntarily step up to the stove. That choice, in fact, might be seen by women as a clue to an often unrecognized value of a feminine art. Despite the men's awakening, however, middle-class women remain the primary audience for cookbooks, and the book necessarily focuses on this large group. Most cookbooks project mainstream expectations and assume a middle-class lifestyle, but they are not labeled "for the middle class only." As agents of our consumer culture, they speak also to American ethnic groups: Italian Americans, Asian Americans, African Americans, Hispanic Americans, and indeed to all working-class Americans, saying, "This is what you ought to aspire to." While aspirations may be difficult to achieve or altogether unsuitable, they nonetheless are presented as goals.

The women in this book are, in the main, white middle-class Americans. The purpose is not to celebrate them to the exclusion of other American women. Rather, *Can She Bake a Cherry Pie?* asks white women to recognize, critically, that this is the world they have inhabited and do inhabit. Whiteness is an unmarked characteristic; whites often live with a strong sense that both culture and race are something that happens to other people. It does not occur to many white middle-class American women that they have a distinct culture that defines them quite as much as ethnicity or other group identity is assumed to define others. For most of the twentieth century, African Americans, as well as immigrants from Europe, Asia, and Latin America, were pressured to adopt the food customs of the dominant culture and abandon their own in the interest of being "American." Elements of the cuisine of other cultures crept into mainstream American cooking only slowly and often without acknowledgment. As this book will show, it has been in the kitchen that a great deal of middle-class culture has been and is powerfully asserted as the American norm. It is time for those of us who, like it or not, are deeply steeped in that culture to look critically, but not solemnly, at ourselves—with our aprons on.

Reading between the lines of the recipes and surrounding texts of cookbooks reveals much about societal expectations and how they change. Women may have been trapped in the kitchen by cultural demands, but they have also found ways to resist them. For some women, the kitchen has been a place they can control as well as a place for expressing something of the private self.

But many have questioned traditional assumptions—that cooking is women's work, that love can be measured by time spent in the kitchen.

The way we cook both reflects and is part of the cultural construct of the moment. Because most of the practitioners of home cooking have been women, the kitchen is a place to study women's lives.

The kitchen begins as a bare room; it is fitted with built-in cabinets, counters, and appliances, but in earlier times it was furnished with free-standing iron stoves, iceboxes, cupboards, and tables. In some present-day kitchens, the refrigerator and the microwave oven are the stars; busy members of the household feed themselves on demand in minutes, not necessarily simultaneously. Other kitchens are full of gadgets—food processors, mixers, grinders, blenders, ice cream makers—a clue that at least one person in the household does serious cooking at least some of the time. In response to this effort, people sit together and share a meal, as they have from time immemorial.

In the past, the kitchen was a center of production, an active part of the family economy. The simple necessity of feeding the family was the motivation for home cooking; the assignment fell to women, who were, in any case, close to home rearing children. Looking back to our rural past from the end of the twentieth century we may envy for a moment the security of rural women, whose role in the family economy was acknowledged and certain. They worked hard, and they knew what they were doing was essential. Their cooking, in its reality and as we nostalgically imagine it, seasons our attitudes and provides a benchmark to which we can compare later developments in the kitchen.

CHAPTER ONE

Mrs. Abney's Ham

THERE WAS A TIME WHEN I ACTUALLY USED TO MAKE BAKED
BEANS FROM SCRATCH, STARTING WITH HARD LITTLE WHITE
beans and molasses and salt pork, soaking and boiling the beans, mixing everything together in a copy of a real New England brown bean
pot, and cooking the beans in the oven all day. I was young, newly married, and knew almost nothing about cooking; I picked the recipe out
of the crisp, unstained pages of my brand new copy of *The Joy of
Cooking*. My baked beans tasted good (after I'd made them several
times I noticed that I had halved the amount of beans and nothing
else, so they were richly sauced). But what impulse drove me, a city girl
whose experience of baked beans was limited to what came from a can
or the little individual brown pots at the Horn & Hardart Automat on
Forty-second Street, to think of doing such a labor-intensive thing?

Like many city dwellers I suppose I was nostalgic about a past
I'd never known. Richard Hofstadter said long ago, "The United
States was born in the country and has moved to the city." Once there,
urban Americans retained an admiration for "the noncommercial,
nonpecuniary, self-sufficient aspect of American farm life."[1] Making
baked beans from scratch was a hands-on way to experience a tiny
piece of the way people once lived. My curiosity about that life was
enhanced some years later when a friend who grew up on a Missouri
farm loaned me his treasured copy of *The Napton Memorial Church
Cook Book*. Through the recipes in this modest, well-worn volume,

published in 1928, I found a way to imagine rural women's lives. The small community of Napton is ten miles east of Marshall, the seat of Saline County, Missouri, where farms spread over the rich soil of the prairie. Here General Thomas A. Smith, formerly of Virginia, established Experiment Farm in 1826 and demonstrated the fertility of prairie land. Settlers attracted by this promised abundance came from Virginia, Kentucky, and Tennessee in the middle years of the nineteenth century to follow his example. Here, according to legend, the land is so fertile that, "if you plant a tenpenny nail there at night, hit'll sprout crow bars by mornin'."[2]

In 1928, Napton had some three hundred residents. The town included Shackelford's general store, T. J. Nicely's grocery store, a big brick school, and the Napton Memorial Church. The rich fields, neatly divided by hedges of Osage orange, produced an abundance of corn and wheat. Beans, parsnips, potatoes, cucumbers, and tomatoes grew in the vegetable gardens. The orchards provided apples and cherries and peaches for pies and steamed puddings.

Missouri in the twenties is far from my own experience. I have to reach into my imagination to see rolling fields and meadows accented occasionally by tall, solitary, narrow houses fronted with roofed porches. The nearest neighbor might be a mile away. Inside one of these houses, somewhere back of the front parlor and the sitting room, and adjoining a dining room sternly furnished with walnut pieces from Sears, Roebuck, is a large kitchen. Its centerpiece is a big wooden table on sturdy legs. The massive black iron stove also stands on legs, leaving space underneath where a cat or dog can find a warm spot to rest. Wood fuels the stove; the supply is ample, but it must be split to fit the stove's wood box.

An oak icebox, insulated with cork and lined with tin, is placed under the window. Blocks of ice in the lower compartment provide the cold. Pond ice cut in the winter is stored in an ice house under the smoke house, where it lasts for months. (In town, an iceman delivers blocks of ice. An ingenious person sometimes cut a door through the wall so that the iceman could deliver fresh ice directly into the back of the icebox without stepping inside and tracking mud and dripping water onto the kitchen floor. A design recommended in *House and Garden* in 1922 was made with slats in the outside door. In winter the slats could be opened, allowing cold outdoor air to substitute for the ice.)[3] The wide porcelain sink with its two drain boards also stands on legs. If a woman is lucky, the men in the family have installed a pump to bring cold water directly to the sink. A linoleum rug in a subdued green and gray plaid protects the wood floor.

In such a kitchen Mary Abney, wife of Hood Abney, a farmer, presided and worked. She and her husband were in their thirties and had two young daughters. All summer long, ripening produce governed her work schedule. When the strawberries ripened, it was time to make jam. When the peas filled their pods in the garden, they must be shelled, cooked, and eaten or put up in glass jars. Later thousands of string beans dangled from the bush requiring picking and stringing and putting up. And of course each year the hogs grew fat and must be butchered—and then it was time to do the hams.

Meanwhile the farm demanded daily work. Mrs. Abney kept her vegetable garden, and when harvest season came, she was ready to feed the extra hands with home-grown meat and vegetables and homemade preserves and butter. "Missouri's eating," boasted the writer of the state's volume in the Work Project Administration (WPA) series,

> is as good as it comes. Boone County ham steaks and red ham gravy, ham baked in milk, barbecued ribs and backbone, authentic country sausage and genuine head cheese; fried chicken and baked chicken and chicken pie and dumplings and chicken soup, eggs from the hen house and bacon from the smokehouse; sauerkraut with squabs, and turnips with spareribs, spring greens from the yard and roadside, and green beans with fat pork—bush beans as long as they last and then long pole beans until frost. Missouri tables are loaded with dish on dish of berries—strawberries, blackberries, raspberries, floating in cream; with Jonathans, Grimes Goldens, Winesaps, Black Twigs, Delicious; apple pie, apple cobbler, apple strudel, baked apples and fried apples; homegrown tomatoes and watermelons and horseradish grown in the country's horseradish center; an endless number of pickles, always including pickled peaches and 'end-of-the-garden'; vast varieties of jellies and preserves; persimmons sweetened and whitened by

frost; popovers, wheatcakes and honey, piping hot biscuits and melting butter and molasses; fruit shortcake always with biscuit dough; cornbread from yellow meal without so much as one grain of sugar.[4]

This mouth-watering description fails to mention the women who achieved this abundance of body- and soul-warming food. The men smoked the hams out in the cold smoke house, but the women made sausage indoors. They made preserves and canned the fruits and vegetables they had raised in their gardens. They tended chickens.

The technological progress that was already altering the tasks of feeding the family in some parts of the country had not yet reached this rural community. Women performed their work much as their mothers and grandmothers had, in kitchens that showed little change. If the pump had not yet been moved indoors, they carried water in buckets from the well out back, which might be two hundred yards from the kitchen door, and heated it on the wood stove. They carried buckets of slops from the kitchen to the pen where the hogs were kept.

These women baked their own bread as a matter of course, even after Continental Baking Company introduced Wonder Bread in 1927. In *The Napton Memorial Church Cook Book*, published in 1928, they shared methods of making yeast and favorite recipes, but offered no basic instruction in bread baking. They had learned from their mothers and would teach their daughters how to judge the temperature of the water that would be warm enough to prove the yeast, how long to knead the dough, and how to tell when it had risen just enough (but not too much). The book included helpful suggestions about fitting the baking into the day's work. Mrs. Emma Francisco started her Salt Rising Bread by scalding a teacup of new milk and pouring over it a half cup of meal while preparing the midday dinner. Set in a warm place overnight, this began to ferment. Early the next morning she added warm water, salt, soda, sugar, and enough flour to make "a tolerable stiff batter." Set in a pot of hot water, it would rise quickly, then she would add more warm water and flour, knead the dough, shape it into loaves, and after the second rising, bake the bread. It would be ready in time for that day's dinner.[5]

The bread supply had to be renewed often; other food must be prepared in season and stored. In the long, bitter winters, Napton women used what they had put up or stored. Cabbage, stored in the root cellar or buried in the ground, was a winter staple. A recipe for Mock Cauliflower—which is really just creamed cabbage—suggests how tired the farm family grew of eating cabbage as the winter wore on.

Some of the cabbage went into relishes like Mrs. Hood Abney's Pepper Hash, which called for "fifteen large onions, twenty-four sweet peppers, five or six hot, two small heads of cabbage, one and one-half tablespoons of salt, two tablespoons of celery seed, three tablespoons of mustard seed, one pint sugar, one and one-half pint vinegar." The directions are brisk. "Mix vegetables together and pour boiling water over them, let set about five minutes, then drain well and mix with other ingredients. Heat to boiling point and seal."[6] The women who used this cookbook would know how to chop all those vegetables and were familiar with the canning process.

All summer the fruit ripened: wild blackberries, purple raspberries, peaches, gooseberries to can in sugar syrup. "In canning any fruit always test your jar by turning it upside down after you have screwed your top as tight as you can. If it runs out the least bit your fruit will spoil," warned Mrs. J. F. Field. To make preserves, fruit could be boiled on the stove with sugar until the juice thickened. Another method spared the cook from standing so long in the hot kitchen; Mrs. I. C. Sydenstricker's energy-saving Suncooked Preserves needed only a tin roof.

> Weigh equal quantities of strawberries or cherries and sugar. Let them stand together over night in a cool place. In the morning bring to a boiling point; put in shallow meat dishes or granite ware and put on a tin roof where the sun will shine on them all day. Keep them in the sun two days, then put them in glass or stone jars without heating.[7]

(This bizarre method of making preserves turned up a few years later in a very different context in the *Most for Your Money Cookbook*, aimed at helping city people eat well during the Great Depression. For the hard-up dweller in a railroad flat, the fire escape and a cookie sheet took the place of the tin roof.)

Meat, too, was preserved to last through the winter—in quantity. Mary Abney gave her recipe:

SUGAR CURED PORK

For 1000 lbs of fresh meat use 40 lbs. of salt, 10 lbs brown sugar, four lbs. black pepper, one-half lb. of red pepper, one-half lb. salt petre. First rub the meat thoroughly, using half the mixture. Take care to rub in especially around the bones and the shank ends of hams and shoulders. Pack in box or lay on table, if the latter; be sure and have some of the mixture on the table before meat is put on; skin side down. Let lay ten days. Second—then rub the remainder of mixture into meat leaving at least 20 days or two days for every pound of meat for the larger pieces, such as hams. Third—Brush off or wash off in warm water, hang up to dry and smoke several days with hickory or apple wood. Sack all hams, putting only one in each sack.[8]

The hams, once cured, lasted. To begin with, wrote Virginia Abney, Mary's sister, who had married Hood's brother (making her Mary's sister-in-law as well), "If the ham is two years old I scrub with brush, cover with water and soak over night. Next morning I cover with fresh water, skin side up and boil from two to three hours. When done the small bone in the hock end will come out. I then remove from water, skin, cover with or sprinkle white sugar and grate some bread crumbs over it, also stick in a few cloves if I want it to look extra nice." Then she baked it in a slow oven for one or two hours, "depend[ing] on how long you boiled it." Her neighbor, Mrs. Marsh Field, sharply disagreed with this method. "Most persons boil ham," she began, but in her opinion, "it is much better baked, if baked right." Baking it right, Mrs. Field believed, required six or eight hours in the oven, which meant stoking the oven all day.[9]

Mary Abney liked to cut inch-thick slices from the ham, put them in an open pan, sprinkle them with brown sugar, dry mustard, and black pepper, cover them with sweet milk, and bake them, turning them when they were half done to brown both sides. No scrap of meat went to waste. "After the ham will not bear slicing," advises Mrs.

George P. Smith, "cut all of it off the bone and grind it and mix with a salad dressing. This is very fine for sandwiches."[10]

The last of a chicken also got honorable treatment. There were chicken croquettes, of course, and chicken patties, which might be elegantly baked in pastry-lined scallop shells. Mrs. Smith called her simple and tasty recipe, "A Nice Way to Fix Cold Chicken." For a dainty and delicious supper dish, she suggested mincing leftover chicken and putting it in a baking dish with "a few cracker crumbs, butter, pepper and salt. Pour cream over it and bake."[11]

Desserts were the pride of Napton cooks. Appreciative eaters, then as now, gave them more attention and acclaim than the chickens, hams, cabbages, and turnips of daily meals. The abundance of the farm allowed Virginia Abney to use the yolks of sixteen eggs for her Gold Cake; if enough company were expected she would make a second cake, using a recipe for Angel Cake that her neighbor Mrs. Murrell provided that called for sixteen egg whites. Both could be served on a summer afternoon with iced tea. An experienced cook like Mrs. J. M. Buntin could create a luscious marble cake, part lemon flavored, part spice cake:

> One teacup sugar, one-fourth cup butter, two eggs, one-half cup sweet milk, two cups Maud S. flour, into which has been thoroughly mixed one teaspoon of baking powder; one teaspoon lemon extract. Beat well together, then from this batter take one teacup of dough to which add one tablespoon of molasses, one tablespoon flour, one teaspoon each of cloves and cinnaman [sic], and one-half teacup seeded and chopped raisins. Place a layer of light batter over bottom of pan. Drop the dark over this and proceed until all is used. Bake in moderate oven.[12]

Mrs. Buntin specified the brand of flour, because flours were not uniform. If a neighbor used Hi Pat or Hummer flour she would have to adjust the measurement to get the right texture to her batter. All three brands were locally produced.

The women might produce a splendid array of such cakes to provide refreshment for a church social or to be sold to raise money for the church, or a political candidate, or some other good cause at one of the auctions that brought Saline County people together to socialize now and then.

To please the children, mothers and grandmothers produced dozens of lemon cookies, caramel cookies, plain sugar cookies, Surprise Cookies, which hid a secret stash of cut-up raisins or dates mixed with sugar and nuts, or Mrs. John C. Patterson's mysteriously named Lept Cookies, a Christmas treat rich in dried fruit, nuts, and spices. Of cookies, of course, there could never be enough. In the middle of the baking section of the Napton cookbook, the editor interrupted with a verse:

> *Oh weary mothers, rolling dough*
> *Don't you wish that food would grow?*
> *How happy all the world would be,*
> *With a cookie bush, and a doughnut tree.*[13]

The next female generation was trained up in the ways of baking early. Mrs. Max Mason had a recipe she called Children's Sponge Cake. "Any little girl can make this," she said.[14] The young cook must have had patience—or help from her mother—to beat the batter by hand for five minutes but, baked in muffin tins, it was ready in ten. Surely the little cakes made a festive tea party for the young cook, her friends, and their dolls.

In order to maintain the right temperature in an iron stove without a heat regulator, women relied on wisdom passed from mother to daughter or learned by trial and error. There were various methods of estimating when the oven was ready to bake. One rule was, "When putting the bread in the oven, it should be hot enough to hold the hand in and count twenty rather quick."[15] Women who preferred not to scorch their fingers used another trick, measuring the temperature by how long a piece of white paper took to turn brown. A recipe for a magnificent Klondike Cake (twelve egg whites and from three to nine egg yolks—"as many as you wish") gave these instructions: "if baked in a coal oil stove, put cake in oven then light it and turn so flame is half red and half blue. It will take one and one-fourth hours or even longer to bake. Put your ear to the pan and if you hear a hissing sound it is not done."[16]

The novice, lacking such experience and judgment, might en-counter disaster. "If the oven is too hot," one cookbook author warned, "the top crusts over before the cake has risen sufficiently . . . with the natural result that the cake cannot rise any more until the interior pressure becomes great enough to break the crust at its weak-est point, which is near the center. When this happens, the dough is forced out of the cracks in unsightly ridges."[17]

Mary Abney may have daydreamed over the *Successful Farming* magazine advertisements urging her to acquire a modern stove, but in 1928 most rural households still did not have access to gas or elec-tric energy. The New Deal's rural electrification project was not launched until 1935. Many Missouri women cooked on a wood-fired range, starting the fire in the morning with crumpled paper, kindling, and pieces of wood, then adding larger pieces when the fire was well started. While cooking, the housewife had to adjust the dampers to maintain the oven temperature and add more fuel "a little at a time, but not in the midst of baking." And, of course, the ashes must be cleaned out every day.[18] Hood Abney liked to be up-to-date, so Mary Abney was one of the first in town to have an electric stove. Neverthe-less, as in many other kitchens, the coal-fired iron range remained, warming the kitchen in winter at little cost, while the electric or gas stove waited like an unfamiliar visitor to be used in warm weather.

To beat the high cost of fuel and to avoid overheating the kitchen in summer, some people put slow-cooking dishes—soup, stew, or cereal—in a fireless cooker. *The Settlement Cook Book* ex-plained this ingenious device: a wooden box about the size of a foot locker (in England it was known as a haybox) was lined with tin, with insets to hold pots and preheated discs. A pot of soup, cereal, or stew was first brought to a boil over the flame on top of the stove, then set in a larger kettle, with newspaper stuffed in the space around it; the larger kettle sat in the fireless cooker, surrounded by more newspaper; the food continued to cook slowly in its own conserved heat. Like today's electric Crock-Pot, the cooker needed no further attention, and in six hours or so, the food was cooked. Anybody could improvise a fireless cooker from a large box or trunk; a skilled woodworker could build a fine one and fit it out neatly inside.[19] Mrs. George P. Smith, recommended cooking cornmeal mush in a fireless cooker: "The longer it is cooked the better it is." After supper, Mrs. Smith put the leftover cornmeal mush in a bowl to set overnight in a cool place. For breakfast, she turned the mush out of the bowl, sliced it thick, rolled it in flour and fried it "to a delicate brown in plenty of hot lard" (another product of the hog).[20]

Not long after the Napton women's cookbook was published, Christine Frederick, a "household efficiency engineer," proved what Mrs. Abney and Mrs. Smith knew without thinking about it. Frederick drew up comparative daily household schedules to demonstrate the time-saving value of the fireless cooker. The woman who lacked a fireless cooker rose half an hour earlier than the woman who had one. Her cooking required attention from six thirty in the morning until six at night; she had to interrupt her housecleaning frequently to tend the stove. Her better-equipped counterpart slept later because she had set the breakfast (probably cereal) to cook all night in the fireless. She left the lunch to cook while she did her housework and cleaned the windows or the silver. She even had three hours in the afternoon for "rest or recreation" while the evening meal cooked.[21] In the 1930s, the fireless cooker had revival, this time because it saved cooking fuel.

In Saline County, achieving efficiency was the subject of much discussion at women's club meetings. Timetables and streamlined kitchens were unheard of, but the rhythm of food production and the cooperation of communities accomplished much. Hired girls and neighbors provided helping hands when the work of preserving was heavy. Women welcomed inventions that would lighten the labor of cooking, and gadgets to make the work easier and faster abounded. Mrs. Abney's mother, as a young housewife, might have heeded an earlier midwestern cookbook that advised women not to ignore the peddler who comes to the door with a collection of kitchen tools. "It is well in all cooking to take advantage of all the modern improvements," said the author, and "oftentimes agents bring things to your door that cannot be had at the stores; if you see it is going to be useful to you, it is well to provide it, as when you want it, you may be unable to find it."[22]

Thus encouraged, and perhaps enjoying a visitor to chat with, the housewife might buy one of the many and various apple corers and peelers. Designed to lighten a major chore of the fall season, these ingenious items came in a variety of designs, some small, some large complicated structures that fastened to the kitchen table with a bracket. Or she might decide on a new, improved raisin seeder, a cherry or olive pitter, or perhaps the bread pail (hand powered by cranking) that won a prize at the 1904 World's Fair in St. Louis. Like today's electric bread machines, the bread pail enabled the cook to knead the dough without actually touching it. She might be tempted by a new improved egg beater; hundreds of inventors patented designs before the Dover Stamping Company's "Dover beater," first patented in 1873, became the standard model. Advertised in the Sears catalog early in the twentieth century, it was still an essential kitchen-shower gift in 1952, when I set up housekeeping. Now my egg beater, displaced by the electric beater and the wire whisk favored by modern chefs, languishes in a bottom drawer.

But more than gadgets, even more than gas stoves and refrigerators, rural women desired radios. Although hog butchering, preserving, and church auctions provided occasional social gatherings, the farm wife spent many hours and days alone. Radio brought voices into the kitchen. In the 1920s, *Successful Farming* carried advertisements not only for radios, but also—in those days before rural electrification—for a small windmill that would generate enough power to run one. The radio provided entertainment and a way to be in touch with the world. It also provided recipes. Advice programs sponsored by the Department of Agriculture or nearby land-grant colleges offered tips on canning and cooking as well as on farming. Kansas State Agricultural College provided advice on everything from raising chickens to cooking and interior decorating.[23] In the early days, local stations had many hours of broadcasting time and few programming resources; they filled daytime hours with chat shows starring women who were themselves housewives, who provided cooking ideas and household hints. These programs, with a format like a neighborly visit, encouraged regular listening. In Shenandoah, Iowa, in 1925, radio station KMA began broadcasting from the seedhouse of Earl May's seed company. Gertrude May, the wife of KMA's founder, was the self-styled radio neighbor. In her daily radio chats, she shared her recipes for Bing Cherry Salad, Blueberry Pudding, and Buckwheat Cakes. She told her listeners about family favorites such as Grandmother Welch's Washington Pie. She explained how she made her Ground Beef Recipe, a casserole consisting of layers of ground beef in tomato sauce, cream and cottage cheese mixed with sour cream, scallions, and noodles—a dish I recognize as a classic party dish of the fifties. On Sundays, May sang for her radio audience.

The success of her show turned Gertrude May from a professional housewife to a busy entertainer. "Because of her busy life helping at the radio station and her church and community service," she hired two local women to replace her in her own kitchen, doing the family cooking. Soon their recipes, too, were heard on the airwaves.[24]

The combination of abundance and hard work illustrated by *The Napton Memorial Church Cook Book* so suits the American ideal, it is no wonder that, looking back from the present, many people regard the cooking it presents with nostalgia. If the oven temperature was difficult to control, the life, from our distant view, looks both manageable and secure. We overlook the backbreaking work much as the Napton women omitted any reflections on these aspects of their lives from their cookbook.

Napton women presented their recipes with pride, but left unstated the satisfaction of accomplishment when the sugar-cured pork, smoked with apple or hickory wood, finally was packed into sacks. They did not mention the silky texture of kneaded dough or the delicious smell of bread in the oven or the crunch of the bread knife cutting through the brown crust and the pale tender inside of a new loaf. When Mrs. Mason wtote, "Any little girl can make this," we can imagine her delight as she taught her small daughter a first lesson in baking, as her own mother had taught her, and as she watched the child's excitement at having made a real cake.

Women cooked with a confidence born of custom, experience, and instinct. They measured in teacups and dessert spoons, and "ten cents' worth of macaroons."[25] Results were less predictable than they are now, and instinct and judgment were correspondingly more important in the making of a cook. But today's anxieties about what we eat—the injunctions to eat locally produced fruits and vegetables, the worries about what was fed to the chickens in their distant artificial environments—were unnecessary. Mrs. Abney knew her hog. Mrs. Murrell gathered the sixteen eggs for her cake, laid by the hens that pecked and clucked in her own hen house and chicken yard.

The farming magazines were full of advertisements for the new refrigerators. Extension Service agents preached the virtues of modern equipment as an aid to efficiency. Agriculture Department economists advised that farm women could earn more money (by selling home-canned products, preserves, and fancy work) in a modernized house. Farm women eagerly embraced these ideas, but persuading their husbands to spend the money was another matter. A wife's labor was not perceived as having any money value; it was free. Most of the time, the man of the house got his tractor first. A philosophical woman might say that the tractor made the work easier and husbands less cranky at the end of a long day. Wives must bide their time.

Their day would come. The new refrigerator would take its place in the kitchen or more likely in the pantry. There it would stand, pristine white, with its motor in a round cage on top, ready to store butter and milk and meat and keep them fresh for days.

Meanwhile, kitchen work—rubbing the hams with salt, sugar and spices, peeling potatoes or fruit, kneading bread every day, shredding cabbage for cole slaw, coring and peeling apples for applesauce and pie—was arduous and constant. Women continued to carry heavy buckets of water from wells that might be two or three hundred yards from the house; most men failed to see a pump in the kitchen as a necessity. By their efforts women provided a nearly self-sufficient food supply for their families and the hired workers who helped to keep the family industry—the farm or the store—going. In their own eyes, they were partners in the family enterprise. Mrs. Abney and her neighbors might have been astonished if someone asked whether they should be doing something more constructive, for what they were doing was essential. It went without saying.

CHAPTER TWO

"We Are Going to Lose Our Kitchens"

THE NAPTON WOMEN CONTINUED TO CURE THEIR HAMS AND PRESERVE THEIR FRUIT IN THE WAYS THEY HAD LEARNED FROM their mothers and grandmothers, but even before the end of the nineteenth century other women had vigorously questioned the old ways of coping with cooking and other household tasks. Dolores Hayden, borrowing a phrase from the feminist journal *Woodhull and Claflin's Weekly*, called it the Grand Domestic Revolution.[1] Beginning a debate that is still going on today, these feminists were less interested in the vote than in economic power. They proposed drastic changes in the way domestic work was accomplished. Among their leaders were two brilliant—and in some ways, prophetic—women, Melusina Fay Peirce and Charlotte Perkins Gilman.

Melusina Fay Peirce, born in 1836, was a woman of undeniably strong views who was not afraid of creating a stir; at the age of nineteen she wrote a long letter to Ralph Waldo Emerson taking issue with his views on religion. Having tasted life in Cambridge in her teens, while visiting her aunt Maria Fay, she made up her mind to study at Professor Louis Agassiz's school for young ladies—the closest a woman could come to a Harvard education in the days before Radcliffe College. Blonde and pretty, as well as fiercely intelligent, Zina Peirce had a steady, unflinching gaze. More than one man fell in love with her before she married Charles Sanders Peirce, a brilliant, eccentric philosopher.

She had grown up in St. Alban's, Vermont, the eldest of seven children of a minister father and a hard-working, devoted mother who firmly believed in woman's separate sphere. Her mother's death at thirty-nine was a defining moment for Zina. "I saw her in her coffin," the daughter wrote, "and I resolved to remember the woe and earthly wreck of her thwarted nature, and never to cease until I saw some better way for women than this which can so horribly waste and abuse their finest powers."[2]

Her marriage to Charles Peirce made her a member of an intellectual elite. Harvard professors and their wives mingled with editors and writers in what William Dean Howells described as a social life "so refined, so intelligent, so gracefully simple."[3] She was not intimidated. Living at first with her parents-in-law, Zina Peirce shared her husband's interest in science and often worked with him. Her agile mind had time to ponder the irony of well-read, intelligent women spending their lives cooking and cleaning. "Educated women," she wrote in 1868, "should seek to produce, not with their hands, but with their heads."[4]

Peirce was conspicuous for her energy and outspokenness. Alice James described her as "a nice woman, if she would only refrain from throwing up her head and glaring at one like a wild horse on the prairies."[5] Her mother had taught her to believe that women had a particular responsibility as moral guardians, and that this included making home so pleasant that men would not be tempted to spend their evenings elsewhere, but Peirce balked at the idea that women must devote their entire lives to this cause. She argued for equal economic opportunity for women and saw the career potential in fields where caregiving skills and other attributes society thought of as female were useful. She predicted that if women were freed from the daily need to put breakfast and dinner on the table—and to provide clean clothes and bed linens and other necessities to the family—they would find an economic niche in retail trade particularly suited to their talents.

To attain this freedom, Zina Peirce devised a scheme that would take much of the housework, including cooking, out of the house. She envisioned—and described in a series of articles published in the *Atlantic Monthly* during 1868–69—a cooperative association organized by women. It would begin with a group of at least twelve (or as many as fifty) women. "Their husbands being willing," they would draw up a constitution and by-laws, and Peirce provided a model.[6]

The association would "furnish the households of its members, for cash on delivery, with the necessaries of life, unadulterated and of good quality, and accurately prepared, both as to food and clothing, for immediate use and consumption, and from the profits of this sale [would] accumulate capital for each individual housekeeper or her family." Cooking, laundry, and sewing would be done by skilled workers under the direction of supervisors who were members of the association. Both supervisors and workers would earn salaries or wages, "the same as would be paid to men holding similar positions."[7] The cooperative would sell its goods and services to members at fair retail prices, and the profits (or losses) would be divided among the members quarterly.

"Every housekeeper," Peirce wrote, "would be sure of getting her money's worth," and "she would be saved all the expense and house-room of separate cooking and washing conveniences; all the dust, steam, and smell from the kitchen, and all the fatigue and worry of mind occasioned by having the thousand details of our elaborate modern housekeeping and dress to remember and provide for."[8]

Peirce predicted that by turning the private tasks of the home into public, paid work, women like herself would be liberated to pursue professions or politics in addition to managing the cooperative. The servants who now did most of the domestic work of the white middle-class household would be gone, their jobs done in a central location by trained, wage-earning women who performed sewing, laundry, and cooking tasks. These women, some of whom might be former servants themselves, would benefit by shorter hours (she recommended no more than eight-hour days) and, she suggested tentatively, might even be admitted as members. Peirce also imagined a future of "houses without any kitchens and 'backyards'" full of clothes-lines. It would take the sound common sense of women architects to design such houses, but this was only one of many special contributions that she expected women would make to society when they were released from their housekeeping prison and became financially independent.[9] In the long run, she envisioned that women working together in such a scheme might pave the way to a classless society.

"Regarding cookery," she wrote, "I believe that, like dress, it will never be what it can and ought to become, until women of social and intellectual culture make it the business of their lives, and"—she launched a flight of rhetoric—"with thoughts unfettered by other household cares, devote themselves, like lesser providences, to its benign necromancy." It seems unlikely that Peirce imagined herself as the sorceress of cookery—her genius did not seem to go in that direction. But some women were talented cooks. She hoped that cooperative housekeepers would appoint one such person as chief cook, pay her well, and see that she was well trained, perhaps even sending her to study in Paris. She may not have been interested in cooking herself, but she liked to eat well. Peirce viewed with scorn the plain home cooking of most Americans. With the bounty of food that America supplies, "What feasts fit for the immortals might grace every table, if we only knew how to turn our treasures to the best advantage—and to think that millions of us live on salt pork, sour or saleratus [baking soda] bread, and horrible heavy pies!"[10] Her classless society would not be without grandeur at the table.

While Peirce spelled out her long-range revolution in the staid pages of the *Atlantic Monthly*, she and her friends began an experiment in Cambridge that she hoped would provide a model. In May 1869, a dozen of the refined and intelligent met to discuss the formation of the Cambridge Cooperative Housekeeping Society. Among them were mathematics and physics professor Benjamin Peirce and his wife, Zina's in-laws; Maria Tyler Peabody Mann, a writer and teacher and the widow of Horace Mann, the famous educator; William Dean Howells, the eminent editor and writer; and several other professors and their wives. At the second meeting it was decided, on a motion from Professor Peirce (probably instigated by Zina), that "the organization of this association be referred to the ladies belonging thereto, together with such others as they may persuade to join them in the undertaking."[11] In pursuit of these "others," the women held a meeting in "the room back of the Post Office" on June 10, attended by one hundred invited Cambridge women. Zina Peirce explained in detail how the association would work and persuasively set forth its philosophy. She promised a variety of appetizing meals, as well as better bread, canned fruits and vegetables, and preserves than her listeners could buy in Cambridge shops. She anticipated an end to the grease and pervasive smells of household kitchens. Her address was published in its entirety in the *Cambridge Press* on July 10 for the benefit of any who had missed the meeting.

The group rented a large house on Bow Street, across from Harvard University, and began by establishing a laundry. Probably most of these families of professional men had a laundress who came to the house once a week; often the ironing was added to the chores of the live-in servant. Some considered sending family laundry out to a commercial establishment to be rather embarrassing. The cooperative laundry, supervised by one of their own, bridged the gap. By July 1870, the laundry, under the supervision of Zina Peirce, was breaking even financially. But the next venture, the store that was to supply provisions purchased at wholesale rates and sold at a fair mark-up to members who would collect dividends from the profits at the end of the year, proved to be a failure. Of the forty families that had signed up as members, only twelve patronized the store. The savings could not be achieved with so small a group. The third part of the plan, a kitchen that was to provide hot meals delivered to members' doors, never materialized. The professors, gentlemen that they were, did not forbid, but somehow kept most of the cooperative's members from active participation. They were willing to indulge their wives to the extent of allowing them to pay dues and go to meetings, but they pulled the rug out from under them when it came time to put the organization's ideas into practice. Their attitude and Peirce's own inexperience undoubtedly prevented the association from having the depth of economic support such a venture required. Quietly mocking the idea, the husbands discouraged Peirce's followers. After scarcely a year, the organization dissolved in 1871, before it ever began meal service.[12]

In the professors' view, their wives, and women generally, occupied a separate particular place in the world. They idealized, and at the same time feared, women. Kim Townsend, in his *Manhood at Harvard*, describes a generally chivalrous attitude in which, as Henry Adams saw it, "the women in [the professor's] lives enjoyed only as much social and political and economic freedom as men allowed." A woman "might well conceive of herself in ways that differed vastly and variously from the ways in which [a man] imagined her, but the quality of her life was largely determined by his perceptions of her."[13] When Zina Peirce and her friends began this cooperative venture, they reckoned without this controlling view.

Harvard professors were no more enlightened than other men. From their point of view, a wife's labor belonged to her husband, and they wanted neither to share it nor to pay for it. In fact, the law of property declared that this was so. The wife of a Harvard professor and the wife of a farmer shared a common disability. Legally, any wife's household work for the benefit of the family belonged to her husband, as did any money she might earn unless she were working on her "sole and separate account." A woman who earned money for the support of the family was not entitled to her earnings—they belonged to her husband. A recognized exception allowed farm women to keep the money they made selling butter and eggs, for example, and spend it themselves, but they had no right to a financial interest in the farm, no matter how much their unpaid work contributed to its earnings. No financial value was placed on women's household work; it was simply an obligation. From the point of view of a husband, Peirce's scheme asked him to pay for services he had been entitled to free.

Many feminists who, like Peirce, raised the demand for the two-career marriage in the post–Civil War period, envisioned women engaged in work that made use of traditionally 'feminine' attributes. Others believed educated women should not be limited at all but instead be free to choose medicine, the law, or any professional career. In either case, they viewed domestic work as servile and demeaning. Immigrant women, uneducated and untrained, filled the servant roles that formerly had been held by native-born local girls; in northern cities like Cambridge, these were mostly the despised Irish. The mistress-servant relationship was often adversarial; Peirce, herself outspokenly prejudiced against the Irish, wrote of freeing women of her own class from the tyranny of "those outrageous little kingdoms of insubordination, ignorance, lying, waste, sloth, carelessness and dirt that we unhappy home-queens have to subdue afresh every day." Moving domestic work into a factorylike setting with women managers, she expected, would substitute "a thoroughly organized, well-balanced central despotism, whose every department is arranged, down to its minutiae, with the most scrupulous exactness, and where lynx-eyed matrons and officers have nothing else to do but to note that each servant does exactly the right thing at the right moment, and knows the place for everything and puts everything in its place."[14] A considerable gap separated Peirce's proposal for immediate action and her idealistic (and vague) long-term view. The distant vision of a classless society was hazy and the short-term benefits to working-class women under the gaze of "lynx-eyed matrons" were not clear.

The *Atlantic Monthly* articles found many readers both in the United States and in England. Letters came to Peirce from readers who hopefully assumed the Cambridge experiment was flourishing and begged for practical advice on how to start their own cooperatives. The *Woman's Journal* wondered in July 1870, "Where Is Mrs. Peirce's 'Cooperative Housekeeping?'" and said editorially, "We still have faith in the plan and believe it practicable."[15] When her articles appeared in book form as *Cooperative Housekeeping* in 1884, the *New York Daily Tribune* predicted that her ideas would be "at no distant day the basis of a domestic reform."[16] Zina Peirce's experiment in Cambridge failed, but her concept continued to inspire other cooperative experiments.

The socialist colony of Ruskin (named after the English social theorist John Ruskin), was established in 1896 in rural Dickson County, in central Tennessee. Inspired by Peirce and by Edward Bellamy, the author of the futuristic novel *Looking Backward*, its founders aimed to collectivize domestic work and assure women's economic independence. The community of more than two hundred people treated women and men equally, "each for all and all for each," as one of them, Lydia Kingsmill Commander, succinctly put it.[17]

Women and men at Ruskin worked for wages; all were required to work eight hours a day except women with young children, who worked five hours. Although women worked at a variety of occupations and some men cooked and worked in the laundry, in general women took the lead in the work they knew best. It was women who organized the communal cooking and dining. Women managers supervised the work of cooking, baking, serving, and cleaning up. Four or five women prepared the ingredients and four people cooked. Fitzhugh Brundage, in his history of the colony, describes the system: "While the food was being cooked, a squad of waitresses prepared each of the twenty-odd tables for the meal." When dinner was ready, "the waitresses divided it into serving bowls and then distributed them evenly among the tables. During the meal, a waitress presided over each table and took care of the needs of the diners. Afterward, each waitress carried a pan of hot water to her assigned table, washed and dried the dishes, and returned them to the proper setting."[18]

In addition to saving time and earning wages for their work, Ruskin women discovered another important advantage of the communitarian approach to domestic work—an escape from the isolation of the single family household. The communal plan provided company while they were working. In addition, they had plenty of leisure time; they organized reading groups and clubs and found ample opportunity for social life.

Women had economic equality, but in spite of the community's lofty ideals, they never attained political equality. Simply moving domestic work out of the home and treating it the same as other paid labor was not enough to change patterns of female subordination. The colony collapsed, "split into irreconcilable camps" by arguments over the status of women, the terms of political and economic stewardship, and the degree of latitude for ideological dissent that could be allowed. Reconstituted as the Ruskin Commonwealth, the remaining members relocated by train to a bleak site near Waycross, Georgia, on the edge of the Okefenokee Swamp. There sickness, fire, and economic misfortune plagued them; in 1901 a sheriff's sale of the remaining assets ended their story.[19] They had hoped to achieve "cooperative affluence," but like the Cambridge cooperative they lacked capital; the land was poor and management decisions sometimes questionable. The women, forced back to their solitary kitchens, particularly regretted its demise.

Thirty years after Peirce's *Atlantic Monthly* articles, Charlotte Perkins Gilman published her manifesto, *Women and Economics*. In the book, published in 1898, Gilman, like Peirce, argued that every woman must be financially independent. More firmly than Peirce she affirmed the concept of two-career marriage. Though she insisted that marriage was important, she argued that the institution of the individual family as an economic unit was a waste of resources. In *The Home: Its Work and Influence*, published in 1903, she summarized the pernicious effect of housekeeping. "Two people, happily mated, sympathetic physically and mentally, having many common interests and aspirations, proceed after marrying to enter upon the business of 'keeping house' or 'home-making.' This business is not marriage, it is not parentage, it is not child-culture. It is the running of the commissary and dormitory departments of life, with elaborate lavatory processes."[20] Only by loosening the grip of domestic work on family life could the family be successful.

Peirce thought women were uniquely suited to certain kinds of work, but Gilman believed that educated women should be free to pursue any professional career. She was a grandniece of Harriet Beecher Stowe and of Catharine Beecher, whose housekeeping manual was the essential guide to order and good management for many women. But to Gilman, the idea that homemaking tasks were the natural province of women was nonsense; to be, as she scornfully phrased it, "queen of a cook-stove throne" was not enough.[21]

After insisting for years that she would never marry, in 1884 she married Charles Walter Stetson, an artist. In March 1885, their daughter, Katherine, was born. But Gilman's attempts to behave like a conventional wife and mother led to severe depression, weeping, and inability to work. When she could work, she contributed articles to the feminist *Woman's Journal* and a column on suffrage to the labor-oriented weekly *People*, at the request of Alice Stone Blackwell. Although *People*'s readers were working class, Gilman's column addressed career women and middle-class women who were trapped in domestic tasks at home.

Her enthusiasm for writing and for feminist politics contrasted sharply with her dismal state of mind when she was at home. In the spring of 1887, pressed by her mother and husband, she went to Philadelphia to become a patient of Dr. S. Weir Mitchell, a well-known specialist in diseases of the female nervous system. She endured his treatment—six weeks of total inactivity and bed rest—and she was sent home with instructions to rest, engage in no more than two hours of intellectual activity a day, and spend as much time as possible with her child.

This was a disaster. Eventually she found her own way back to health when she got out of bed and resumed her career as a writer and speaker on questions concerning labor and women. She left Walter and went with Katherine to California, where she moved in with a lifelong friend, Grace Channing. After living apart for several years, she and Walter separated amicably and divorced in 1894. Walter later married Grace Channing. Katherine Stetson spent much of her youth in the care of her father and stepmother, a fact frequently used against Gilman by critics of her radical ideas (a negligent mother could not be trusted, they argued). In 1900 Gilman married her cousin, a friend and correspondent of many years, George Houghton Gilman.

Writing early in the Progressive era, Gilman based her argument for freeing women on progress. If men worked only for their families, she said, they would still be building houses out of logs, hanging hides on the walls, and hunting their food. Progress occurs through specialization and organization, and the housewife, "blinded by her ancient duty, fails in her modern duty" to bring housework up to date. "Each woman, learning only from her mother, has been able only to hand down to us the habits of a dark, untutored past." And while the farmer feeds his livestock scientifically, on the best advice of the Bureau of Agriculture, "humaniculture has no Bureau."[22]

She proposed that cooking, cleaning, and child care, like any other occupations, be treated as business. Women whose talents lay in cooking or child care could follow their bent, and other women would be free to be writers (like Gilman), architects, lawyers, or doctors, according to their abilities. Groups of families would hire women to perform the work and women managers to organize it. Gilman imagined kitchenless homes with centralized community dining service and child care, but hers was a thoroughly professionalized model.

She dismissed cooperative communities as "high-minded idiocies." Instead, she advocated something similar to the "family hotel." People would live in their own apartments but take their meals in a common dining room, and housekeeping services would be centralized.[23]

Many of her contemporaries condemned family hotels, and in fact apartments in general; they associated them with boardinghouses, which were not always respectable. They suspected that to live in such close proximity with other people was morally risky. Gilman, however, saw the possibilities of getting rid of the arduous, time-consuming work of maintenance while preserving the privacy of the family.

She admitted—without much sensitivity—that if cooking were done as a professional service, people would have to give up expecting their every preference to be met, but she offered as compensation that they would develop an appreciation of a wider range of good cooking. Like Peirce, she thought that a good chef would provide better meals than an untrained woman or a family cook.

For those who might react with horror that this scheme smacked of socialism, Gilman said soothingly, "There is no cause for alarm. We are not going to lose our homes nor our families, nor any of the sweetness and happiness that go with them. But we are going to lose our kitchens, as we have lost our laundries and bakeries. The cookstove will follow the loom and wheel, the wool-carder and shears." Then, in homes that were not "declassed by any admixture of industry whatever," she predicted, "the family life will have all its finer, truer spirit well maintained; and the cares and labors that now mar its beauty will have passed out into fields of higher fulfillment."[24]

Both Peirce and Gilman were scornful of the present and optimistic about the future. Peirce's feminist reform focused on the narrow issue of getting rid of the drudgery she hated; she believed that the business model would successfully displace it. Gilman's was a grander scheme; she rejected the idea of the family as an economic unit while affirming it as a cultural institution; she argued that equality in marriage is possible only if each partner is economically independent. In Gilman's vision, freeing women from the prison of home was a necessary step toward a socialist utopia like the one Bellamy described in *Looking Backward.* As a charismatic speaker much in demand on the lecture circuit, she preached Bellamy's ideas as well as her own.

Peirce and Gilman were bound by the class system they lived in and, more than they acknowledged, by gendered expectations. Neither they nor their followers suggested that men take responsibility for a share of domestic work. They believed that women trained in a particular trade would do a better job than the unskilled, poorly educated immigrant or black household servants who did everything. Neither showed much sympathy for the working-class women who actually performed most of the sewing, washing, ironing, and cooking. In some places where families organized communal dining rooms, servants, seeing the threat to their livelihoods, reacted by exerting the only power they had—all the household employees threatened to quit if the cooks were fired.

Peirce, who accepted that women of her own class would be willing to work at their supervisory tasks only three or four hours a day, proposed that they require not more than eight hours of the workwomen—a very short workday at that time. In the Reconstruction-era South, she imagined a role for freedwomen, who might even share in some of the profits. But her real passion, like Gilman's, was reserved for freeing women like herself. Peirce and Gilman were not alone. Reva B. Siegel observes in her study of the legal aspects of women's household labor, that as middle-class women slowly gained access to public work suitable to their education and class, these opportunities "encouraged many women who joined the [feminist] movement . . . to define emancipation of 'the sex' as that which would secure for the movement's middle-class members the privileges enjoyed by men of their social class. Freedom from labor associated with family life was one such privilege."[25]

As city people, Gilman and Peirce based their schemes on the geographical closeness and convenience of city life. Followers of their ideas came up with ingenious schemes—insulated boxes for delivering hot and cold food, and even a design for a cluster of buildings with a little railroad to transport meals. But as public transportation expanded, the middle classes moved to the suburbs. This might have been the opportunity to develop small communities designed from the start around shared facilities. Instead, the overwhelming trend was toward separate, self-sufficient homes, each with its own kitchen and its own yard, and eventually its own washer and dryer. Corporate interests were firmly opposed to shared services; after all, if thirty families shared a single stove (even of restaurant quality) twenty-nine possible sales were lost.

Peirce's cooperative idea was tried in various places around the country. Neighborhood cooperative dining clubs started up, usually with twenty or thirty members who rented a house in a convenient location where the women took turns preparing dinners. Some men thought it was worth sacrificing the home-cooked meal. In 1907 in Carthage, Missouri, the women who were planning a suffrage convention talked of a future in a world without private housework. One husband urged them to hurry. His wife, he said, "is always cooking, or has just cooked, or is just going to cook, or is too tired from cooking. If there is a way out of this, with something to eat still in sight, for Heaven's sake, tell us!"[26]

But communal dining clubs failed to take hold. They had their roots in the communitarian socialism of Bellamy, Charles Fourier, and Robert Owen, and the mere whiff of socialism unnerved many Americans who associated it with free love and lax morals. Clubs seldom lasted more than a few years. The Mahoning Club in Warren, Ohio, was an exception; it kept going from 1903 until 1923.[27] In Northampton, Massachusetts, in 1927, Ethel Puffer Howes, in an attempt to provide jobs for women and services to the community, organized the Institute for the Coordination of Women's Interests. The institute provided cooked food, delivered from a community kitchen (over two thousand meals in one year), housecleaning service, and child care. It lasted only six years. This experiment, like other communal ventures, fell victim to the same fear of socialism that took its toll on earlier cooperatives. In the post–World-War I Red Scare, Howes's institute and others that were part of the women's movement were labeled communist and regarded with suspicion.

In New York City in the 1880s, Philip G. Hubert had organized eight cooperatively owned apartment hotels, calling them "Hubert

Home Clubs." These were not modest residences; the apartments had as many as twelve rooms. Apartment hotels such as these, designed for the well-to-do, were fashionable in the city for a while; the apartments were grand but had small kitchens, and the hotel dining room was available whenever residents chose to use it. Today, some residences for senior citizens have adopted a similar model. The idea has also been adapted for the rich: a private "gated community" of large expensive houses bordering a scrupulously maintained golf course has a restaurant and an extensive take-out menu for its members, although each house has a large and well-equipped kitchen. Country clubs offer meals in an atmosphere that is somewhere between the dining club and a public restaurant, but these are coexisting alternatives to serving meals at home.

The market value of home cooking remains undetermined. The institutionalization of dining seems for many people to lack something. It may be the opportunity to choose food and prepare it just the way the family likes it. It may, for the person who cooks, be the opportunity to dabble, even if only occasionally, in the kitchen. It may be that eating dinner every night with the same friends becomes tedious. Or it may be something more insidious. As Brundage suggested about the failure of the Ruskin community, the experimenters "underestimated the challenge of uprooting conventions of domesticity that were bound up tightly with capitalism itself."[28]

Gilman's proposals for centralized cooking and home delivery took root in a form she never imagined. Commercial food services met the needs of consumers, delivering meals to subscribers for a profit, first by horse and wagon and then by motor delivery wagons. The path was opened that eventually led to the widespread delivery of pizza and Chinese food. People seem willing to accept the sacrifice of minute personal preference for the sake of convenience. The proliferation of take-out food in our own day expanded far beyond Gilman's wildest dreams. Capitalism found ideas in the cooperative experiments and turned them into profit.

Technology for the home kitchen has provided other alternatives to cooking. Frozen complete meals began with the infamous TV dinners first marketed in 1954 and grew to occupy huge areas of freezer space in supermarkets. The cooking, done far from the home kitchen by paid workers, followed recipes devised by professionals, according to standards of uniformity and quality, if not of imagination or individual preference. Commerce and technology, rather than local associations of people with a common purpose, provided the centralized kitchen. Huge food corporations like General Foods, H. J. Heinz, and National Biscuit Company took many cooking jobs out of the home kitchen and sold the finished product back to the consumer. And still the home kitchen did not disappear.

Gilman and Bellamy imagined a society in which science and progressive ideas would free women from the kitchen. But as the twentieth century unfolded, women were not freed from the kitchen. Instead, they were invited to confront it—on modern scientific terms.

CHAPTER THREE

The Kitchen Laboratory

IN 1896, TWO YEARS BEFORE CHARLOTTE PERKINS GILMAN'S *WOMEN AND ECONOMICS*, FANNIE FARMER'S *BOSTON COOKING-School Cook Book* appeared, marking a new era in cooking. The housewife in the kitchen entered the field of science—without leaving home.

In the last decades of the nineteenth century Americans were infatuated with science. The scientific model expanded to include the social sciences. Classification, organization, and measurement were imposed on everything in sight. Melvil Dewey invented a decimal system for classifying all knowledge that would govern the arrangement of American libraries for a century. He believed it would last forever. The University of Chicago established the first department of sociology in the United States, and the *American Journal of Sociology* began publication. In 1899, Ellen Swallow Richards, a chemist educated at Vassar and M.I.T., launched a series of conferences of people working "for the betterment of the home" at Lake Placid, New York, a popular meeting site for progressive thinkers.[1] From these meetings a new science was born and named "home economics." Richards led the way in scientific research on housekeeping, nutrition, and sanitation. The American Home Economics Association was founded in 1908, and home economics became an academic discipline. At land-grant universities with schools of agriculture, home economics departments were established to train increasing numbers of women students. Wary of female professors in traditional science departments, university administrators used home economics as a convenient place to segregate women scientists and keep them from competing with men. At Cornell, the only women to achieve the rank of full professor between 1911 and 1960 were in the home economics department. "In a flash," writes Margaret Rossiter, "a woman chemist could become a home economist, a physiologist, an instructor in 'hygiene,'" or find herself shoved into administration as a dean of women.[2] Applying their knowledge of chemistry and biology to this new field, the women brought scientific structure and exactness to housekeeping, including food planning and cooking.

The science of cooking emanated from universities, where home economics flourished alongside other practical sciences like agriculture. Home economics programs trained women primarily to become teachers of home economics in schools and colleges, but as an academic discipline it had its researchers and its publications. Under its influence, the skills of homemaking ceased to seem instinctive. Traditionally, women had learned to cook from their mothers. Now cooking, like child rearing, became something one studied, trusting the advice of an expert over one's individual judgment.

So cooking went to college. The home kitchen did not disappear, as Gilman had predicted. Science might have provided an escape; instead, it moved into the kitchen. While women scientists in state universities developed the field of home economics, efficiency experts trained in engineering used technology to streamline the solitary housewife's kitchen work.

Fannie Farmer might have become one of the women who earned a chemistry degree if it had not been for her ill health. The daughter of a Medford, Massachusetts, family, she contracted a paralytic illness (probably polio) while she was still in high school and was forced to give up her plans for college. Like many young women of her time, she became a mother's helper in the household of a family friend. At thirty-one, looking for a way to earn a living, she entered Boston Cooking-School. She was a star student and remained to become a highly successful teacher. In 1893 she became the school's principal.

Red-headed and enthusiastic, Fannie Farmer was famous for her cooking lectures and demonstrations. Cookbooks were considered risky publishing ventures then. She persuaded Little, Brown and Company to publish *The Boston Cooking-School Cook Book* in 1896, but the publisher insisted that she underwrite part of the cost.

Like the university-trained home economists, Farmer deplored inexactness. After years of teaching practice, she was able to set down recipes clearly and simply and, most important, she insisted on precise measurements. Fannie Farmer became famous as "the mother of level measurements." She failed to see the charm of the old recipes that called for a piece of butter the size of a walnut, a pinch of sugar, a teacup of flour. The successful *Boston Cooking-School Cook Book* (soon—and still—known familiarly as "Fannie Farmer") educated American cooks to understand that a cup is exactly eight ounces, and in Farmer's uncompromising language, "a teaspoon is a teaspoon, levelled flat." But measurement was not the only indication that scientific methods were being applied to cooking. Farmer knew chemistry and believed that knowledge was essential both for her students in the classroom (some of whom were training to work in other women's kitchens) and for the thousands of students she would never see, the users of the cookbook. So in its opening chapters she explained food and cookery in scientific terms. She identified protein, water, starch, and sugar by their chemical symbols and definitions; she explained the scientific principles behind the action of air, moisture, and heat. She also advised on healthy diet, recommending, for example, that "brain workers should take their protein in a form easily digested" (fish and eggs), but the "working man" could eat corned beef, cabbage, brown bread, and pastry without fear of overtaxing his digestion.[3]

Out there in the cities and towns and villages, the American wife daily confronted the task of cooking. If hers was to be a perfect American family, her husband, and her children must be perfectly fed. But the perfect meal was elusive. Women who got by on instinct (sometimes with dismaying effects) were, it might be said, cooking at random. Women who lived far from the female relatives who might have shown them how to knead dough for bread or make gravy without lumps turned to cookbooks for guidance. Immigrant women knew well what they had learned from their mothers and grandmothers but mainstream American culture scorned ethnic cooking; assimilation included learning what was decreed to be wholesome American cooking.

You can skip the chemistry lessons and still learn how to cook from Fannie Farmer, but her approach to cooking as a matter of learning a range of very particular skills is pervasive. She began with grocery shopping, a serious enterprise. For the novice, Farmer gave sensible and uncompromising advice on what to buy and when to buy it. In selecting a fish, she suggested, "Examine the flesh, and it should be firm; the eyes, and they should be bright." Each vegetable has its proper (and noticeably New England) season, and only at that time was it worth eating; Farmer considered buying produce out of season a waste of money. Although peas "appear in the market as early as April, coming from Florida and California," they were high in price and, she declared scornfully, "hardly worth buying, having been picked so long." Better far to wait for the fresh native New England peas of June. Similarly, the markets might provide corn from June until the first of October, but beware—"Until native corn appears it is the most unsatisfactory vegetable."[4]

Timetables for boiling vegetables, alarmingly long to modern eyes (one to two and a half hours for string beans, twenty to thirty minutes for spinach) and time-and-temperature tables for baking everything from beans to partridge to wedding cake (a fruit cake, steamed for three hours before baking) provided concise information at a glance for the more experienced cook.

But science, while it increased the precision of the process, did not yet save many steps. Time was a major ingredient in many recipes. Farmer's instructions for making stock—the basis for many of her soup recipes—occupy two pages and begin with an awe-inspiring list of tools:

> Soup-stock making is rendered easier by use of proper utensils. Sharp meat knives, hardwood board, two purée strainers having meshes of different size, and a soup digester (a porcelain-lined iron pot, having tight-fitting cover, with valve in the top), or covered granite kettle, are essen-

tials. An iron kettle, which formerly constituted one of the furnishings of a range, may be used if perfectly smooth. A saw, cleaver, and scales, although not necessary, are useful, and lighten labor.[5]

These mighty weapons aided the cook in cracking and sawing beef bones, extracting marrow from within the bone, and other surgical operations home cooks today are unlikely even to contemplate. If today we decide to make our own soup stock, as some serious cookbooks (such as the elegant vegetarian compilation, *The Greens Cook Book*, by Deborah Madison) recommend, we require nothing like the weaponry Farmer called for. When we have made a batch, we can store it in the freezer. In Farmer's day, the only way to keep stock for a while was to boil it up every day to prevent it from spoiling.

Under the guidance of scientific cooks like Fannie Farmer, the kitchen became a laboratory. Farmer was uncompromising in her instruction. The encrusted, blackened old iron kettle was banished.

Farmer insisted on chemistry and nutrition, but she was also subversive of her own science. She allowed her students, and the readers of her cookbooks, to play at being artistically creative. In 1907, Georges Braque, Fernand Léger, and others were showing Cubist paintings in Paris. The 1907 edition of *The Boston Cooking-School Cook Book* offered a recipe for Berkshire Salad in Boxes. The cook preparing for a luncheon party built little boxes out of crackers stuck together with egg-white glue, tied a red ribbon around each one, and filled them with chicken salad. The patience and manual dexterity necessary to achieve enough of these for a luncheon table would rival a watchmaker's; we can only hope that the guests were lavish with their admiration, if not delight, before they destroyed these delicate morsels with one whack of a fork.

Similar patience and delicacy of touch must have gone into another pièce de résistance, Monte Carlo Salad.[6] This bridge club treat began with grapefruit, celery, and apple, mixed with mayonnaise, and arranged on a plate. Then came the tricky part: "Outline, using green Mayonnaise, four oblongs to represent playing cards, and denote spots on the cards by canned pimentos or truffles; pimentos cut in shapes of hearts and diamonds, truffles cut in shapes of spades or clubs." Then the joke: "Garnish with cold cooked carrot and turnip, shaped with a small round cutter to suggest gold and silver."

These were architectural extravaganzas, but the food was plain, even bland (Farmer encouraged simplicity, especially for beginners). A challenge for the ambitious cook was not in the use of exotic ingredients or subtle spicing but in contriving presentations that, though almost too good to eat, were soon consumed. The ephemeral nature of cooking is almost insisted upon by delicate, complex structures that the diner, after a moment's viewing, willfully smashes like a child knocking down a pile of blocks.

If cooking was a science (occasionally embellished by art), some people envisioned housekeeping as a business. In the nineteenth century, Catharine Beecher and Harriet Beecher Stowe had written advice on home management. In 1912, in a book with the uncompromising title *The Law of the Household*, Eunice Beecher (a Beecher by marriage) set forth rules for running a household like a business. She claimed that her plan promised wives some of the empowerment at home that their husbands enjoyed in their business or professional work.

While watching a building contractor and his crew who were working on her house, Beecher had a revelation. "I saw a vision of women's emancipation through system," she recalled. In her view, the woman of the house was like the contractor, a manager who trained and supervised a staff of workers. Like Melusina Fay Peirce, Beecher did not believe that servants could be trusted to do anything properly on their own. Neither did she think women of her own class were much more knowledgeable, but she believed they must learn. She firmly insisted that the mistress must know the correct way to do everything about the house.[7]

Beecher saw home management as an unpaid career and hoped that women would prepare themselves for it, just as their husbands prepared themselves for careers in business. Otherwise, she said contemptuously, a woman of her class was nothing but a social butterfly. Beecher's manual gave detailed instructions for every sort of household activity. She set forth rules for everything from polishing brass to managing house guests (who were not to be encouraged to bring children; if they did, the children were to be banished to the top floor and not seen). "Mrs. Beecher," observes Faye Dudden, "found security and revenge in creating a domestic world of perfect order and ruthless neatness in which she was undisputed ruler."[8]

Servants performed some of the labor of cooking, under the direction of their mistresses. Many of the mistresses, as Beecher understood, knew little themselves and considered finding a good cook a stroke of great fortune. But between 1896, when the first *Boston Cooking-School Cook Book* appeared, and 1927, when the recipe for Monte Carlo Salad entered it, the number of servants diminished by about half. In 1890 the ratio was one servant to every ten households. In 1920 it was one to every eighteen households, and this trend continued. It meant that many daughters of prosperous households would have to fend for themselves after marriage. As a new wife my mother was one of that breed who, in the commonly used expression, "didn't know how to boil an egg." Bessie McElroy, my grandmother's Irish cook, had ruled the kitchen with an authority that did not invite questions, let alone participation. New brides like my mother (whose private school education included French taught by native speakers but not home economics) depended on cookbooks to tell them how to cook vegetables and how to tell when a chicken is done by wiggling its leg or pressing a finger to its breast. They looked for advice on judging the ripeness of a melon, brewing coffee, and removing coffee stains from linen tablecloths.

As the hired household labor force diminished, the general housekeeping or cooking manual increasingly had to assume that the middle-class wife was on her own. She wouldn't need to worry about training inexperienced help; instead she would have to learn how to organize her own work, make the best use of new technological "servants" like mixers and gas stoves, and entertain without a cook and a waitress.

Technology, in fact, was crucial in the transition from hired Irish cook to the middle-class woman alone in her own kitchen. In 1926 a small cookbook called *Electrical Homemaking* advised, "Experts on electrical housekeeping say that every modern kitchen should be supplied with these aids—refrigerator, cooker, dishwasher, kitchen motor, and ventilator."[9] The age of technology was reaching into the kitchen. Piped gas to fuel gas ranges and refrigerators was available in cities. Propane gas in tanks made ranges and refrigerators possible in some rural kitchens in the 1920s. But until the Roosevelt administration's rural electrification program in the late 1930s, only one in ten farms had electricity.

Prosperous families had refrigerators. They were expensive to buy as well as to operate, but according to their advocates, they promised "absolute freedom in marketing."[10] Trips to the grocery store could be less frequent, and even in summer, food was far less likely to spoil. Although 1920s refrigerators look small to us and lack freezers, they provided welcome reliability to people who had dealt with melting blocks of ice and rapidly spoiling food in warm weather.

The new stoves had temperature controls. The little tricks women had used to judge the temperature of the oven—and to maintain it in spite of the drafts that blew through the wood stove to keep the fire going—were a thing of the past. The electric oven had three settings—high, medium, and low—that eliminated the guesswork.

But, as the historian Ruth Schwartz Cowan has pointed out in her book, *More Work for Mother*, these new gadgets, installed in individual households, still required a woman to keep them stocked and running. If grocery shopping was less frequent, delivery services also diminished, and women drove cars to fetch the family groceries. In addition, manufacturers happily told their customers, the new stoves and refrigerators didn't just simplify, they made new wonders possible. Progress led not only to greater ease but to greater demands.

Recipes for jellied salads and tricky desserts, developed by home economists in the test kitchens of refrigerator companies, soared to unprecedented heights of complexity. It would have been hard to resist the temptation to try these wonders, at least once. An advertisement in *Time* magazine in 1928 shows a new General Electric refrigerator standing squarely on its four elegantly curved legs on the fashionable checkerboard linoleum floor. The refrigerator is square and stubby; its outside hinges and door handle strongly resemble the hardware on its wooden, ice-chilled predecessor, the icebox. The motor sits on top, a latticed, hermetically sealed cylinder. And the text claims, "Just an ordinary grapefruit after a brief stay in a General

Electric Refrigerator becomes a rare treat. Just a simple salad acquires the best-hotel air when it is chilled to the point of crispness. . . . The modern housekeeper has also found to her surprise that with a General Electric Refrigerator it's just as easy to make a luscious mousse as it used to be to make an uninteresting rice pudding."[11]

By this time the great food manufacturing companies had taken over much of the production of food that once had occupied wives. Continental Baking Company made bread, Armour prepared hams. Fleischmann's had perfected the difficult task of producing yeast that would behave consistently. Commercially prepared products were available in city grocery stores. The role of women in producing food—canning, baking, preserving—was different. On the farm, even the scale of food preparation changed as the tractor altered the pattern of farm work, drastically reducing the number of farm hands that had to be fed. The federal government, through its farm agencies, campaigned to turn farm women into homemakers. The women, as Katherine Jellison has shown in her book, *Entitled to Power*, did not want to be "released" from productive labor, but the prescriptive literature was aimed to make them "scientific" consumers of goods instead – and leave the patriarchy stronger than ever.

The great goal was consistent results. The model was science. The scientific approach not only regularized cooking, making the product more predictable, and increasing the cook's confidence, but also, not coincidentally, granted a certain seriousness to what women were doing in the kitchen. Cooking no longer depended on instinct (a female characteristic) and folklore (the province of women). Nutritionists weighed the value of the elements of food composition. Domestic scientists in laboratories determined through experiment the exact formulas for successful food preparation. Stark black-and-white photographs illustrated for the uninitiated the properties of successful and unsuccessful muffins. Nothing was left to chance.

The woman in the kitchen—no longer supervising paid workers—now patterned her work on a masculine model, the chemist in the laboratory. The kitchen itself, formerly like any other room, furnished with painted wooden furniture, and a stove to cook on, in the 1920s came to look like a laboratory, its furnishings white and scrubbable. The tall Hoosier cabinet, a freestanding piece of furniture; had pull-out porcelain work surfaces, compartments, some especially designed for particular items of cooking equipment, and bins for dry ingredients like flour. Originally made of oak, by 1922 it was available in porcelain-coated steel. It hinted at the organizational possibilities of the built-in modular cabinets that would come later.

Marie Meloney, the editor of a well-known women's magazine, *The Delineator*, argued that the home could benefit from the application of principles from both science and business management. She created an organization called Better Homes in America; her lofty aims were to foster improved household management and encourage people of moderate income to build sound, efficiently designed houses. Her plans also depended on a woman who would devote herself to learning and practicing management, decorating, cooking, and—of course—shopping.

Herbert Hoover, then secretary of commerce and a professional engineer, was an enthusiastic supporter of Meloney and the scientific approach. In 1923 he designated Better Homes in America a public service organization connected with the Commerce Department and named himself as its president. Better Homes was not just a promoter of efficient housekeeping, but a representative of the United States government as well. Good homemaking had patriotic implications.

"The future history of America will be shaped in large measure by the character of its homes," Meloney announced. "If we continue to be a home-loving people we shall have the strength that comes only from a virile family life. This means that our homes must be attractive, comfortable, convenient, wholesome. They must keep pace with the progress made outside the home."[12]

Meloney organized affiliates in cities across the nation. To help people keep pace, the affiliates presented exhibitions of model homes. In Atlanta, the model home was furnished in genteel style. The living room had Wilton rugs and a framed reproduction of the famous painting familiarly known as Whistler's Mother. Further cultural enhancement was signaled by a piano and a set of the *Book of Knowledge*. The dining room boasted a mahogany dining room suite. In the kitchen a shining Frigidaire, which at $550 cost nearly as much as the piano or the dining-room furniture, dominated the scene. The Atlanta Better Homes organization set forth its goals and those of its clientele in a pamphlet available at the exhibition. The organization existed "to assist and encourage *home makers and home builders.*" The homemakers' tasks (not counting actual cooking and cleaning) were noble: "To strengthen *home life* and make it attractive. . . . To improve the *home environment,* thereby strengthening the child. To increase the efficiency of the wage-earner of the house."[13]

Some people ignored the Better Homes advice, and others rebelled against it. But Marie Meloney's Better Homes in America program sought to impose a national culture that prized manufactured goods and prints of great masterpieces as signs of respectability and good taste. The style was decidedly respectable and middle class; the implicit message was that this was a style to which all Americans should aspire.

By the mid-twenties, Marie Meloney had moved on to the New York *Herald Tribune,* where she established the Herald Tribune Home Institute to test new ideas about housekeeping and cooking before they were published in the newspaper. She hired Lillian Gilbreth, an efficiency engineer specializing in time-and-motion study, to design a scientifically correct kitchen. (Gilbreth was also the mother of twelve children, two of whom later immortalized the family in the 1948 bestseller, *Cheaper by the Dozen.*)

The design of kitchens had not really been a matter of interest in the past. Now, as professionals turned their attention to home design, creating formulas for decorating and recipes for good taste, the models they drew on for kitchen design were efficient factories and scientific laboratories.

Time-and-motion study originated in the methods developed by Frederick W. Taylor and Frank B. Gilbreth (Lillian Gilbreth's husband) to increase the productivity of factory workers by improving spatial layouts and minimizing unnecessary movements. "Taylorism" was a dirty word to workers who found themselves pushed to work ever faster and gospel to managers who wanted more product for less money. But, as the application of science to human tasks, it suited the belief in science and progress that characterized the times.

Lillian Gilbreth based her design first on the principle that every kitchen should be tailored to the height, taste, and working habits of the woman who would use it. (Decades later when I had an opportunity to design my own kitchen, I discovered how much easier life became when the counters, like me, were a few inches higher than average.) Her time and motion studies led to a second principle, "circular routing" to eliminate unnecessary steps.

Earlier research by Martha Van Rensellaer, a home economist at Cornell and homemaking editor of *The Delineator*, had measured the inefficiency of old-fashioned kitchens by putting a speedometer on a housekeeper in a kitchen in Ithaca, New York. In 1923 the National League of Women Voters elected Van Rensellaer one of the twelve greatest women in the United States. Gilbreth, to cut down the miles of walking, placed the sink, stove, and refrigerator at the points of an imaginary triangle, thus reducing the distance between them.[14] Her design was put into practice in the Herald Tribune Home Institute kitchen. Shiny white modern appliances and a handsome checkerboard floor of black and white linoleum tile added to the scientific atmosphere of this "home laboratory laid out by the country's greatest home engineer, which takes the drudgery out of household tasks and gives the homemaker that dignity and joy in her responsibilities which rightfully belong to the most important profession in the world."[15]

When the kitchen was completed, the Home Institute staff tested it. First one of them made strawberry shortcake in "a typically haphazard kitchen" (the kind most people lived with). Then she followed the same recipe in the new Gilbreth-designed kitchen. The results were gratifying: in the new kitchen, with furniture, equipment, and storage arranged according to scientific principles, the cook took only 64 steps in the course of making the shortcake; to do the same task in the old-fashioned kitchen had required 281 steps.[16]

Gilbreth believed "that the business of running a house demands a well-planned 'office' just as surely as does any business run by a man," so she included a "housekeeper's planning desk" in the model kitchen.[17] Here the housekeeper planned menus (with her cookbooks and recipe files at hand), paid bills, and telephoned orders to the grocer and butcher. "Personal marketing should be done twice a week, but the telephoned grocery order can never be entirely dispensed with."[18]

The modern scientific housewife had an ear on the world. "The Institute feels that the radio has a definite place in the modern kitchen, contributing not only to the happiness of the housekeeper but to her efficiency, since it enables her, without leaving her work, to listen in on much of the useful and interesting information about her job which is now being broadcast." Besides, said Meloney, diverting momentarily from science, the radio "glorifies many of the common tasks of the kitchen by a musical accompaniment" which made work go more easily. "It has long been realized that marching soldiers forget their fatigue when the band is playing . . . and the arm that beats a cake does so with less realization that it is work if the movements are timed to the beat of a waltz."[19]

Now that the woman who presided in the kitchen was not a servant but the mistress of the house, whose husband went to an office, practiced a profession, or worked in a laboratory, the space was redesigned, not only to make the work easier and more efficient, but to grant dignity to its practitioner as well. Middle-class women were encouraged to play at science and business in the kitchen.

Manufacturers of stoves and refrigerators and producers of processed foods were eager to make a place for their products in this new scientific and servantless kitchen. They hired women with degrees in home economics to develop recipes using their products and to advise on marketing strategies that would attract consumers. Christine Frederick, a university trained home economist, made a profession of serving as a consultant to business on what women want—and on how to make them want it. She published articles and books of advice for women homemakers and also advised those who marketed things to women. Advertising men and corporate officials who had new products to promote or were looking for ideas to develop sought out Frederick as an adviser and speaker.

In 1929 she gathered the ideas she had expressed in speeches and papers into a book called, without guile, *Selling Mrs. Consumer.* The confidential tone she took in her advice to the industry on food marketing is blatantly patronizing to women, but male executives listened to her. "Mrs. Consumer" became the passive object of their sales pitches and the target for their newly developed products. Frederick not only identified the buyer, but also suggested ways to pitch the advertising directly to her. Shopping, which in Fanny Farmer's scheme was a means to an end, now took on the aura of a professional activity. Recognizing a fresh fish when you met one and knowing when to buy peas were simple tasks compared to making wise choices among the vast and complex array of products available, and advertisers were all too ready to help.

"Mrs. Consumer"—I imagine her as that cute, slim, eager woman with a tiny starched apron who decorated the pages of magazines and cookbooks—wanted convenience. She wanted relief from the task of thinking up new menus. When manufacturers were peddling time-saving items, she was busy—but busy with what? With a bridge club, tea parties, or children; certainly not a career. Her husband earned the money; she provided the unpaid services and was exhorted to spend prudently and conserve resources. She needed to be told how to enjoy—and spend her housekeeping money on—the expanding array of processed foods at her disposal. The rural farm women had been producers but urban wives were solely consumers of goods.

The technological advances that began in the late nineteenth century raised possibilities for variety and quantity of processed foods from cream of mushroom soup to Fig Newtons. Manufacturers learned to produce on a large scale—canned foods in the twenties, frozen fruits and vegetables in the thirties, frozen fish sticks and other "ready-to-eat" items of the fifties, cake mixes, instant rice and macaroni—and improved packing and transportation of an ever-widening variety of fresh produce. Supermarkets like Piggly Wiggly (the first store opened in Memphis in 1916) and King Kullen (the first of its "monstrous stores" opened in Jamaica, Queens, in 1930) started a trend toward today's giants; the supermarket consumer is emblematic of the age.

People had to be persuaded to use what the food industry produced. A new abundance of production required a new approach to cooking. It was no longer a question of following the seasons and the farm's produce, preparing for scarcity by putting food by—smoking meat and preserving fruit. Mrs. Consumer's "job" was to support the national economy by buying its products, providing a market for processed foods, fresh meat and produce, and new kitchen equipment.

Middle-class Americans were no longer supposed to save, they were supposed to spend. Warren Susman has pointed out that the new abundance meant that Americans "must develop new values in keeping with that new status. Leisure was rapidly becoming almost as important as labor," and that meant learning "a pleasure ethic, if not to replace, at least to put beside, [their] work ethic."[20]

Fannie Farmer had stuck to cooking, chemistry, and nutrition. Marie Meloney and Better Homes in America took the scientific model devised by the home economists and expanded it by providing a laboratory setting and the language of noble purpose. But while these advisers conferred the status of science on the work, they took away initiative. Theirs was the science; they laid down the rules. The woman, professional as her kitchen might look, was only encouraged to follow the recipes. She was demoted from a carrier and transmitter of tradition and knowledge to a worker trained to execute tasks.

Cooking became more efficient and less arduous. When all the emphasis was on modernity, few people noticed—or lamented—the loss of tradition as a force in cooking. The professionals promised much, but as women lost the skills of bread making and the knowledge behind their grandmothers' cooking, they also lost the confidence that had produced the Napton women's cookbook.

Decades later they would find it difficult to reconstruct , even with recipes, the dishes their grandmothers had made. Like dance, cooking in those earlier days had not been carefully recorded; everyone assumed a certain knowledge passed on through oral tradition. A friend told me how she had tried many times to make a certain stew from her grandmother's recipe; it just didn't taste right. Finally she figured out that if she caramelized the sugar called for in the recipe she could achieve the taste she remembered so well.

Not all cookbook authors made science a way of life. A more comradely approach was that of Irma Rombauer. She was not a scientist, nor did she have a reputation as a fabulous cook. Instead, "the sort of cooking Irma's friends most remembered from her was not dazzling culinary virtuosity but seat-of-the-pants improvisation." Her biographer Anne Mendelson writes, "it was her nature to do most things in a blitz of energy, charm, and impatience to be doing something else. Cooking was no exception."[21] Nevertheless, in 1931, Rombauer gave a cooking course to the members of the Women's Alliance in her Unitarian church in St. Louis. The recipes she taught became the basis for the first edition of *The Joy of Cooking*, a small book, privately printed. The title alone spelled a break from science and efficiency. The recipes were intended to enable even a beginning cook "to make palatable dishes with simple means."[22] Five years later Bobbs-Merrill published an enlarged *Joy of Cooking* and Rombauer was on her way to becoming, if not a household saint, then a reasonably good substitute for that somewhat mythical mother who once taught daughters to cook. Her philosophy is pragmatic, without grand claims of science or patriotism. As she said in a later edition, "Cooking is a daily job, it may be a daily chore, why not make it a daily adventure?"[23]

The Joy of Cooking was my mother's guide and became mine. Budgets are never mentioned, and Rombauer resisted providing menus to people whose tastes she had no way of knowing. (She eventually bowed to pressure from her relatives and her publisher.) The recipes are there and so is a personality that—for those it appeals to—soon seems like a friend. Who can forget Rombauer's definition of eternity: "a ham and two people"? Or her attribution of a Cheese Custard Pie to "a vile-tempered cook named Marguerite"?[24]

Rombauer, as Mendelson points out, represents a generation of cooks who had the resources of the food manufacturers at its disposal. Her gravy was enhanced with bouillon cubes and Kitchen Bouquet and she delighted in canned condensed soups. She liked Italian food but, like most American cooks of her time, she was not accustomed to cooking in olive oil. Some of her best recipes were, as she was, of German origin. She was an enthusiastic cook who hoped her readers would be the same.

The scientific approach of the home economists denied or abstracted the immediacy of food and cooking, removed it to a distance from the world of human relationships. They never mentioned the gentle sizzle of sliced leeks cooking in butter in their recipes for vichyssoise or conjured up the elegant associations of that wonderful soup that is so utterly simple in its construction. So something was missing. Several things. Rombauer brought back at least two of them: humor, and the sense of neighborliness that pervades *The Napton Memorial Cook Book*. Not that she was cute about it; Rombauer was never that. But her style, emerging from that course she taught for her friends in the Women's Alliance, is not that of an instructor. She shares what she knows, and says what she thinks. To my surprise, I've encountered people who don't like her book or her sense of humor. But on reflection, that's natural enough, for she has a personality.

As science, business, or technology, cooking was no longer a democratic feminine discourse. The idea that cooking talent was an innate, highly prized quality of certain women was overshadowed by scientifically tested, printed instructions. Cookbooks necessarily standardized the recipes that had once been highly individual communications among women. They set standards of uniformity for white middle-class Americans. At the same time, they implicitly set white middle-class American culture as the standard to which other Americans should aspire.

The emphasis of standard cookbooks on Americanization turned people away from the cooking of their ethnic background toward an American style that blended multiple traditions, often losing the best elements in the translation. The Better Homes in America movement equated good home management with patriotism. And as writing about food and nutrition spread in the pages of daily newspapers and magazines, and as cooking and homemaking instruction took to the air waves on local radio stations, the people who wrote and talked began to introduce another ingredient, a dimension of responsibility for family happiness. This emphasis on psychological needs increased when the prosperous twenties were followed by the hard times of the thirties.

CHAPTER FOUR

Stone Soup

SMART, STREAMLINED, SCIENTIFIC KITCHENS HAD LITTLE
RELEVANCE IN DEALING WITH THE HARD TIMES OF THE
thirties. It mattered little how many steps the cook must travel between the refrigerator and the stove if the refrigerator was empty and
the fuel bill unpaid. Ingenuity and thrift took precedence over exactness and modernity.

The old European folk tale "Stone Soup" can be read as a recipe
for survival. In the story, a traveler appears in a village and cooks up
a fine, nourishing soup, beginning with nothing but a stone and some
water. One person grudgingly supplies a carrot, another an onion, another a potato, and soon the Stone Soup is a delicious and nourishing meal.

Recalling his childhood in the Great Depression, a successful
physician told his own children, "We were never hungry—my mother
made soup."

Between 1929 and 1932, eleven million people lost their jobs
and many people went hungry. Many others avoided hunger only because women exercised frugality and ingenuity. Those who had been
poor all along knew the tricks of "eating tight," but women abruptly
bumped from the middle class, who were accustomed to ordering
roasts from the butcher by telephone and even hiring a maid to cook
them, had to learn to make their families feel well fed on a small,
uncertain budget.

The family, as an institution, was called on to maintain the psychological welfare of its members. Instead of stressing science and efficiency, cookbook, magazine, and radio advisers on homemaking wrapped their advice to women in a blanket of family welfare. Psychology provided a new rationale for domesticity. According to Warren Susman, "by the early 1930s all the devices of the media, the energies of psychology and social science, were enlisted in a major effort to revitalize and reassert the primary importance of the family. Scientific marriage counseling was born as a profession. The importance of child-rearing in a strong family setting was reemphasized," and significantly, "the role of women was again to be found in the home primarily and not outside it."[1] These trends, already prevalent, gained more power as people dealt with fear and shame.

The *Ladies' Home Journal* carried a series of profiles of families called "How America Lives." In the manner of a curious neighbor, the editors peered at families in communities from Brooklyn, New York, to Cucamonga, California, from sharecroppers in Warren County, Mississippi, to the family of a major meat packing magnate in Chicago. Their style in decorating, their cars, their jobs, their children's health and personalities, and—most intimate of all—their budgets were revealed. Regardless of region or income, the families selected by "How America Lives" managed their households in traditional ways; husbands were in charge of cars, wives of kitchens. Their relationships were clearly affectionate and child centered. Their morale was high, chiefly as a result of constant vigilance. The woman who kept the budget under control and managed the family's psychological welfare earned the magazine's highest praise: "a good manager."

But the meaning of being a good manager had changed. The middle-class woman who, in the 1920s, had been told to play at being in business, managing her home as her husband managed his enterprise (and helping her husband advance by providing social support in the form of dinner parties) was now told that when her husband was out of work or fearful of losing his job, she must provide the emotional strength that would enable the family to go on. And food was an obvious morale builder and comforter. Apple pie would make her husband feel like a man.

This may have come as a shock to women who had grown up

with ideas about being a "New Woman," having a career, being eco-nomically independent and spiritually free. But proportionally more women than men lost their jobs in the early years of the Depression, and wives of unemployed men found the doors closed against them when they went looking for work. The reemphasis on the family was accompanied by widespread exclusion of married women from paid employment. A new policy allowed only one spouse to work for the federal government, and the Work Projects Administration, while em-ploying some women in clerical positions, focused on building high-ways and airports, creating work for men. School boards fired their married women teachers. Unofficially, community disapproval dis-couraged married women from "taking jobs" that ought to belong to male breadwinners. Many Americans ignored evidence that most married women who worked did so out of necessity and often as the sole wage-earner for a family. Even the president of the Massachusetts Women's Political Club said, "They (women in paid jobs) are desert-ers from their post of duty, the home."[2]

In time, and in spite of public opinion, married women regained their place in the labor market and gained a little: by 1940 some 25 percent of American workers were female. Several factors may have been involved: unemployed husbands, postponement of children, and extended families living together to save money and share in child care.[3]

Nevertheless, the prevailing view was that their activities at home, of which cooking dinner was an often-cited example, were more essential than anything else women might do. Even the obligations of citizenship took second place. After women won the right to vote, many states still did not allow them to serve on juries. In those states that did permit women jury members, it was customary that they ask and be granted permission to be excused because of their domestic responsibilities—and most women did. George Wickersham, as chair-man of the National Commission on Law Observance and Enforce-ment, opposed compulsory jury service for women because "they have other duties that seem to me to rise far beyond the heights of serving on juries."[4]

Criticizing Wickersham's lofty pronouncement, Jennie Loitman Barron pointed out in a League of Women Voters pamphlet that even when the number of women working outside the home increased, "children have not gone, in greater numbers than before, breakfastless to school. There is no recorded increase in the burning of soups."[5]

In 1937, Judge William Clark of the U.S. District Court in Newark, New Jersey, began running a jury school to train prospective jurors, particularly women. By December he had instructed twenty-five hundred people. But the strong sense that women should be at home cooking dinner continued to get in the way of their civic duty. Eleanor Roosevelt, who firmly believed that jury service was every citizen's responsibility, attended a meeting at which representatives of various women's organizations discussed women's service on juries. One woman mentioned that her husband worked hard running his business, and her daughter also "was obliged to go to business." It was her job as housewife, the woman said, to see that the other members of the family were well taken care of, and not to add to the family expenses. She needed to be free during the day to shop for groceries and cook meals for her husband and daughter.

"She asked to know, then, how she could serve on a jury," reported Mrs. Roosevelt in her newspaper column, "My Day." Mrs. Roosevelt saw no problem. "The answer is, of course, that the family as a whole must recognize the fact that jury service is a duty and, putting their heads together, find a solution. Someone could be brought in to cook the necessary meals—$3 a day is paid for jury service. Of course, it would be nice to keep that money but if this is a duty, it is worth doing well." She added a gentle poke: "Perhaps the members of the household not serving on a jury might look in the icebox for sufficient food to keep them going, even to making themselves a cup of coffee and a boiled egg, if necessary."[6]

But Eleanor Roosevelt was ahead of her time in this as in many of her ideas. At a time when a Gallup poll showed that 82 percent of Americans believed that married women should not work outside the home, the primary duty of woman seemed to be domestic. During the Depression, many American women managed to feed their families despite dire economic circumstances. They accomplished this whether or not they were also doing paid work. The magazines, newspapers, and cookbooks seldom acknowledged the double burden but constantly assured them that what they did in the kitchen had great importance to the psychological welfare of their families and the nation.

The little miracle of "stone soup" occurred in many kitchens. Some of the most economical, and delicious, soups have always been those that the cook concocted from whatever happened to be around. She could feel smug in the extreme thrift of using up what would otherwise go to waste—the limp carrots, the last stalks of celery, a few beans. Embellished bit by bit by half an onion, a couple of potatoes, the leftover wings of a chicken, brightened with a few spinach leaves, picked from the vegetable garden or a remnant of the bunch from a store, and with a pinch from a jar of dried parsley, this unremarkable conglomerate became a sustaining lunch or dinner.

In the *Most for Your Money Cookbook* of 1938, the authors, Cora, Rose, and Bob Brown (Cora and Bob were mother and son, Rose was Bob's wife), suggest an imaginative variety of soups, "mostly made out of things we throw away."[7] Like Stone Soup, many of the Browns' soups were based on nothing—the water in which vegetables have cooked, simply seasoned and thickened with potato or rice; the remains of a can of tomatoes that was opened for something else; a bouillon cube (they appeared on the market in 1931) or a can of chicken broth or consommé. A woman who saved leftover or damaged vegetables and bones and scraps of meat and dried celery leaves for seasoning could make soup at virtually no cost.

The Browns had lived in Japan, China, France, Germany, and Brazil; everywhere they collected recipes and observed customs and kitchens. The *Most for Your Money Cookbook* was an early title among some fifteen cookbooks they published between 1935 and 1960. It took a strong position on the side of the individual and against the big food manufacturers. A friend showed me her copy; it got her through the 1930s, the early years of her marriage. I opened it where it fell open, to the recipe for Green Split Pea Soup. The page was stained and stiff from lying close to the stove and the cook. The ingredients are familiar though, like any soup, this one has many versions expressing the personalities of different cooks.

Some people flavor split-pea soup with salt pork or make it the last appearance of a ham bone or turkey carcass. But the Browns didn't assume that a roast turkey or baked ham had preceded the soup; they could count on nothing so lavish. Theirs requires only a solitary slice of bacon.

This cookbook gave much credit to old-fashioned soups, "Whole meals in themselves which built the sinew of our nation." Fondly remembering the old iron stockpot on the back of the coal range that converted meat scraps, trimmings, and leftovers into broth, they had to point out that "soup meat [is] now as dear as beefsteaks used to be." For the cook who couldn't afford such luxury, the Browns contrived their own nourishing, substantial recipes, inspired by European traditions. Coriander and Bread Soup called for lamb kidneys and sheep brains, but if even these inexpensive innards were unavailable, an egg scrambled and cut in strips could substitute. Scotch Broth was made with stock, not lamb. They gave two versions of buttermilk soup, one thickened with rice, one with egg, accompanied by one of their frequent and forthright political statements: "Buttermilk should sell for less than half the price of fresh milk. Although in some places milk trusts hold up the price of buttermilk, independent dealers sell it for as little as 4¢ a quart."[8]

The Browns' Spanish Garlic Soup calls for ten cloves of garlic and very little else—olive oil, bread, water, and hard-boiled eggs for garnish. Something very like it is still a signature dish of Iruña, a Basque restaurant in Cambridge, Massachusetts, where the soup's delicious warmth and fragrance make customers forget cold, dreary February days. The Browns' similarly warming, satisfying Bread and Cheese Soup would, with a salad, serve as an end-of-the-week supper, using up the last bits of dried-out cheese and stale bread.

Soup stock may have looked like a sounder investment than the Wall Street variety. At any rate, stock was a mark of a thrifty housewife who used every scrap of food to good advantage. In the old days, the stockpot simmered for hours on the back of the wood or coal range; the expense involved (as Fannie Farmer's instructions demonstrate) was in time and labor, not money. Ida Bailey Allen, a food expert of the thirties and forties, pronounced the old-fashioned stockpot impractical for the modern kitchen. Allen knew what she was talking about; she dispensed cooking advice and recipes through her school of cookery in New York, articles in *Ladies' Home Journal* and *Good House-keeping*, a syndicated newspaper column, a radio program, and, in the course of her career, fifty-six published cookbooks. She had no intention of giving up the idea of homemade stock. Instead, she speeded the process. Her meat soup stock simmered a mere five hours (Fannie Farmer's required eight). Her vegetable soup stock, based on pinto beans and potatoes, cooked in an hour and a half, and for extra thrift she recommended using the cooked vegetables to make bean hash.

Making stock—or for that matter, making soup from scratch—was an old-fashioned skill, no more real to many of Allen's urban, modern listeners and readers than the stone soup of the folk tale. Campbell's canned condensed soups had been around since the turn of the century; by 1904, the company advertised twenty-one kinds of soup. Cream of mushroom and chicken noodle came along in 1933. Advertisements and promotions made canned soup seem essential. It had become a staple.

The Browns were not impressed. In their view, shopping was political. They welcomed an opportunity to outwit the corporations as well as to save money. In one of the frequent jabs at big business that spiced their advice, they grumbled, "The canned soup manufacturers are the ones who now fatten on our soup needs," and moved on.[9]

But while the Browns took their stand against the corporations, most of the literature of cooking enthusiastically embraced canned soups. "Mrs. Consumer" had not entirely disappeared. Those who didn't choose to chop, simmer, and stir were encouraged, even in those hard times, to open a can, add water—or, more lavishly, milk—and warm up their soup. Working wives (there were many, despite public disapproval of married women working outside the home), and women heads of households needed all the help they could get. Husbands, even those who were out of work, might "help out" around the house, but they generally didn't see housekeeping as their responsibility. It was a rare man who did the cooking if there was a woman around.[10] Canned soups were a boon to women whose time was scarce.

Campbell's twenty-one varieties included both plain and fancy soups, not only the ubiquitous tomato and cream of mushroom but chicken gumbo and Philadelphia pepper pot. The original pepper pot, as James Beard describes it in *American Cookery*, was hawked in the streets of Philadelphia by women cooks.[11] It began with a veal knuckle, simmered with herbs and water for two and a half hours. The broth that resulted was combined with tripe, onions, and Tabasco or red peppers and simmered for another hour and a half. Then the cook made tiny balls of chopped beef suet and flour and water, and dropped them in the soup along with some finely diced potatoes. In her famous *Settlement Cook Book*, first published in 1901, Lizzie Black Kander (the title page always, with propriety, called her Mrs. Simon Kander) advised her readers to begin with the manufactured Philadelphia pepper pot, but to improve it with cans of concentrated pea soup and tomato soup, as well as two cups of milk.[12]

Home economists and other recipe makers—to say nothing of the soup manufacturers themselves—couldn't leave well enough alone. They tinkered, dreaming up combinations or adding ingredients. Kander used canned mock turtle soup merely as a base for her own, adding tomato soup, homemade soup stock, paprika, cloves, salt, and Madeira wine, and, of course, thin slices of lemon and hard-boiled eggs—the whites chopped and the yolks left whole, floating in the tureen—as garnish. If all this seems like a lot of trouble, consider the real mock turtle soup. Like pepper pot, it requires cooking veal bones and water with vegetables. After three and a half hours the stock is ready for the addition of sautéed ground beef and garlic, Worcestershire sauce, sugar, and browned flour for thickening.[13]

Irma Rombauer, already famous for *The Joy of Cooking*, boasted in *Streamlined Cooking* (1939) that "a finer product than canned soup was never produced." In this book, which stressed the use of commercially produced foods, she displayed a chart of "Soup Mergers" dressed up with fancy names. Cooperstown Soup combined a can of vegetable soup and a can of cream of tomato soup. A can of chicken gumbo and a can of vegetable soup added up to Soupe Paysanne.[14]

Just because a cook opened cans did not mean she had to forego attempts at elegance—the cans were just the beginning. Rombauer offered a soup that would grace the fanciest dinner party, wittily named Boula Boula.[15] This begins with two cups of green peas (frozen peas, first marketed in the thirties, were useful for this recipe) cooked, puréed, and then reheated with two tablespoons of butter, two cups of canned green turtle soup, and one cup of dry sherry. (This was not a soup for the thrifty.) Each serving is topped with two tablespoons of whipped cream, then placed under the broiler.

My grandmother and my mother often served black bean soup, the kind that came in a can, with a spoonful of sherry laid in the bottom of each soup plate to mingle with the hot soup; they always decorated it with chopped hard-boiled egg and a thin slice of lemon. Only when I moved away from New York City to a region where Campbell's black bean soup wasn't sold did I discover that it could be made from scratch with dried beans. Soup as a first course gives a meal a leisurely and lavish air, but Depression-era cookbooks pointed out that it also took the edge off appetites. When money was scarce, the main course that followed could be smaller and simpler without leaving people feeling hungry. A sturdy soup, as the Browns knew from their travels abroad and as many immigrants to America were aware, makes a fine main course itself and leaves the family feeling well fed. Whether contrived from the contents of cans or cooked for long hours from basic ingredients, it carries an aura of comfort.

Canned or homemade, soups are not only thrifty in ingredients, but can be prepared with the most minimal cooking equipment. For people who found themselves living in cramped quarters with poorly equipped kitchens, this was important. The ideal modern kitchens of Marie Meloney's high-tech imagination were so much pie-in-the-sky for Americans trying to get by. Not many people were building glossy new kitchens in the thirties. In cities, people rented whatever they could afford and felt lucky if it included any kitchen at all. The Community Health Association in Boston, in a pamphlet, *Low Cost Food for Health*, prepared "for the many women with small incomes who are struggling to provide wholesome food for their families," offered "Menus for Use in Homes without Ovens," in addition to menus for cold and hot weather.[16]

Pierre Franey, who went on to a glorious career in cooking, remembers coming from France to the United States in the desperate days of 1940. "In my mind's eye," he recalls, "I can still vividly see the one furnished room on West 75th Street in New York City I occupied. . . . There was a two-burner stove. I had a black iron frying pan, an iron Dutch oven and a two-quart kettle . . . [I] had brought with me from my home in France [as only a Frenchman would] a good paring knife, a chef's knife and a whisk. I also had the trussing needle my brother had fashioned out of copper. There was a French pepper mill, too, and a vegetable peeler. And that was about it."[17] Excellent knives and pepper mills were not then considered the necessity in American kitchens that they are today, and most American women had never seen a trussing needle. Franey, a fine chef, cooking teacher, and writer, was one of those who would teach Americans the importance of these things.

Making do with what was available was, in the Depression years, the only possible course for many. It was pursued, no doubt, with more or less ingenuity or frustration. Nobody knew how long the Depression would last, and anxiety was everywhere. Electric and gas appliances made many aspects of food storage and preparation easier, but the cost of fuel was a serious consideration for families operating on a small budget. Cookbooks gave tips on conserving power. Women cut vegetables in very small pieces so they cooked faster; they soaked cereal overnight so the cooking time would be shorter. One book suggested cooking potatoes or beets in the bottom of the double boiler while stirring the pudding in the top. Someone invented a "Depression pot" divided in sections that enabled a cook to warm three leftovers on the same burner.[18]

The fireless cooker had yet another renaissance, this time not to keep the kitchen cool or for efficiency but to keep the electric and gas bills under control. Once a soup or stew was started and brought to a boil on top of the stove, the pot, nestled in the fireless cooker, would hold the heat and the soup would go on cooking for hours without using a penny's worth of fuel.

A woman who was a good manager might tuck the soup pot in the fireless cooker and go out to do her grocery shopping. Here, as in soup making, spending time could save money. When, in the twenties, homemaking experts like Marie Meloney and Lillian Gilbreth recommended having a telephone in the kitchen, many city women had acquired the comfortable habit of calling the grocer to place orders which were delivered by a boy using a cart or a bicycle with an enormous basket. Now, when thrift was the watchword, the experts advised women to resist the temptation to pick up the phone. Instead, they recommended at least twice weekly personal visits to the grocery store and the butcher. "The housewife who takes an interest in her job of being the spender of hard and uncertain earnings," said the Browns, who devoted a chapter of their book to marketing, "has to be a keen detective, as well."[19] Thrift and careful shopping were the fashion, even for the rich. Elizabeth Wilson, one of the women interviewed for *Ladies' Home Journal*'s "How America Lives" series, was married to the head of a major Chicago meat packing company; she had a staff of six servants. Seeking to be exemplary, she did "her own marketing daily and insist[ed] on paying Wilson and Company full price for every prime roast and leg of lamb from the best the huge organization offers."[20]

A woman, whatever her circumstances, was a better shopper if she sized up the chickens by personal inspection and saw for herself whether the fruit was past its prime. At the same time, she could cultivate her relation with the grocer and the butcher and, as a favored customer, get better service and better bargains. So she would exchange friendly good mornings, ask after the grocer's wife and children, talk about the weather, flirt mildly with the butcher as he ground her hamburger or trimmed and sliced her calf or lamb liver, cajole him into throwing in some beef bones or chicken feet to flavor the soup. For a woman who stayed at home, alone or in the company of small children, these seductive—but safe—encounters (hardly anyone actually ran away with the butcher) added spice to dull days.

The butcher shop offered items seldom seen in today's supermarket display cases. "I think particularly of sweetbreads, brains, liver, hearts, and a delicacy called 'lamb fries,'" Dorothy Sterling remembers from her days as a young New York wife in the thirties. "Know what they were? Lambs' testicles!" The *Most For Your Money Cookbook* recipe for Mountain Oysters (another euphemism for this delicacy) tells how to skin, wash, and parboil the lamb fries, roll them in cornmeal, and fry them golden brown. They were served on toast, sprinkled with lemon juice, nutmeg, and Tabasco. "Lamb fries," said the

Browns, "have no waste and are great value in meat, for usually they're sold cheap because the squeamish are afraid to buy them or to ask the butcher, 'Otto, how are your lamb fries today?'"[21]

Both nutrition rules and cultural expectation made some kind of meat almost indispensable on the American dinner table. In a conspiratorial tone, the Browns shared their secrets. Calf hearts, "all meat and no waste," for instance: "For a dime we buy two of them, and make them into ritzy dishes we wouldn't be ashamed to set before Oscar of the Waldorf." They recommended stuffing the hearts and braising them with onion, carrots, herbs, and peppercorns. They explained how to stew sheep trotters "a la poulette" and lamb tails, "a real delicacy."[22]

Women with energy and time could design their shopping for maximum savings. Being a "smart shopper" meant checking the newspaper ads for specials at the still-novel "cash-and-carry" stores that were the predecessors of supermarkets. It meant buying milk in these stores rather than having the milkman deliver it in his horse-drawn wagon and taking the bottles back to collect the nickel deposit. It meant buying day-old bread and avoiding prepared meats (bologna and hot dogs), which were expensive for the food value they contained.[23] The *Most for Your Money Cookbook* had plenty of suggestions: if you live in a big city, buy from the pushcarts, cannily using the knowledge you've gained from that book about judging the ripeness of a melon or the freshness of the beans; shop for fresh produce late on Saturday, when prices on goods that were likely to spoil over the weekend would be greatly reduced; at home, dry celery leaves to use as seasoning later on, and use the liquid in which vegetables were cooked to add flavor to gravy.

The smart shopper planned menus to make maximum use of every penny spent—not only watching the specials but also using imagination about cooking unfamiliar meats, innards, pigs' feet and tails ("right down to the squeal," the Browns said).[24] *Good Housekeeping* provided menus "to suit your pocketbook." For a summer Sunday dinner, the magazine suggested tomato juice and crackers to take the edge off appetites, followed by sliced canned corned beef as the main dish, accompanied by mashed potatoes and peas just as if it were roast chicken. Other dinners featured cabbage rolls, scalloped tuna fish and potatoes, and of course, meat loaf.[25]

Thrifty shopping was the good business management that had been prescribed to homemakers in the twenties, adjusted for hard times. But hard times required something more. Food is more than nourishment for the body; the belief in America as a land of plenty finds expression in meals. In times of plenty, the groaning board, the massive roast, multiple side dishes, and lavish desserts are testaments of personal and national success. But in hard times, the *appearance* of plenty at the table becomes important. Soup could supply the illusion of abundance as well as the reality of a full stomach. Corned beef hash became more festive in the company of broiled tomatoes. Ann Batchelder, a food columnist for *Ladies' Home Journal*, suggested garnishes: "Pickled walnuts sometimes make a Hamburg steak feel like a Porterhouse."[26] (Somehow just capitalizing "hamburg" and calling it a steak dignified it, too.) And dessert, as every child knows and few grown-ups really forget, can be wonderfully cheering.

Ida Bailey Allen advised on everything—nutrition, shopping, pressure-cooker cooking. Her radio and newspaper audience wrote to her asking for help. In her Depression cookbook, *Ida Bailey Allen's Money-Saving Cook Book*, she answered some of the questions her readers and listeners posed in their letters—questions that reflect the anxiety of the times. "Should a family go without meat?" they asked. Like the Browns, Allen firmly believed that families need not go without meat, even on a tight budget. "Take the butcher into your confidence," Allen advised, "and tell him you want a *cheap cut of high-grade meat!*"[27] She, too, advocated the "clever use" of innards—items unfamiliar, and therefore unappealing, to middle-class Americans. The smart shopper watched for specials and explored the uses of lesser known foods, overcoming the family's hostility to anything new and strange by offering favorite side dishes and familiar desserts. With careful planning, Dorothy Sterling recalls from her experience as a young married woman in New York City, even an occasional splurge on lamb chops was possible.

"How can I fill my family up and not appear stingy?" one of Allen's correspondents asked, voicing a concern she shared with many others. Allen and other food writers responded with hundreds of recipes for filling dishes, "stretching" small amounts of meat with rice or oatmeal, substituting cheese or eggs or beans. Families on relief, like the O'Briens (another "How America Lives" family) had a dollar a day to feed seven. "So the O'Briens don't pick their own menus," the magazine reported, "they eat whatever the chain store cut-price specials happen to be that day or week." Honey O'Brien bought canned vegetables on sale and evaporated milk. She picked up what was available from the federal surplus commodities depot, adding eggs and butter and dried prunes to the family's diet.

But perhaps the most poignant question Allen received was, "Can a man out of a job afford pie?" If the right to have pie is not in the Constitution, it certainly is embedded in American culture. The ingredients for a pie crust and a few apples and some sugar for filling, enhanced, if possible, with cinnamon or nutmeg and a touch of lemon juice and grated peel, produced, in the hands of a reasonably skillful cook, an apple pie that not only tasted good but made a man feel as if he were still entitled to something. And while it's true that Allen's advice put the burden on the wife to make her husband and the children feel as if all is not doubt and chaos, it's equally true that there was real satisfaction for the cook in being able to do something, however short-lived (for undoubtedly the apple pie vanished quickly), to make the world feel steadier.

For the many women who were wage earners (whether from choice or necessity) as well as wives and mothers, thrifty shopping that depended on taking extra time in order to save money must have added to their burdens. The work of feeding a family—budgeting, planning, shopping, and cooking—to say nothing of cleaning up after the meal—took time as well as thought. For those men who suffered shame at finding themselves unemployed, the last thing they wanted was "women's work."

While women used their ingenuity to create dinners that gave the appearance of plenty and their energy to exercise thrift in shopping, they still worried about balanced diets. They knew more about nutrition than their mothers had. The careful planner considered the need for adequate protein, minerals, and "fuel foods"—as they were called—carbohydrates and fats. The discovery of vitamins in the twenties had further complicated the matter. Manufacturers played on nutrition anxiety. Any skinny child might be diagnosed as "run down" or undernourished; the makers of Bosco and Ovaltine promised mothers that their chocolate-flavored powders, added to milk, would provide adequate nourishment. An advertisement for Ovaltine promised to "build up your child this summer, [in] a way that adds a pound a week while curbing nervousness, too," while Bosco claimed to increase the "growth value" of milk by 30 percent.[28]

Scientific meal planning meant that a day's main meal always included a vegetable or two, and potatoes, bread or rice, as well as meat, fish, eggs, or cheese, but only concern for the morale of husband and children accounts for the inevitable presence of a home-cooked dessert. Pie, cake, pudding, even Junket or Jell-O, did much to compensate for any insufficiencies at dinner. The meal was complete, with all its courses and a familiar treat at the end, and for a little while an aura of security surrounded the family.

While much of the emphasis was necessarily on the daily feeding of the family, the desire for more festive and sociable occasions existed and brought with it its own anxieties. "Should a family entertain while in debt?" Allen's audience wondered. Behind the question were two worries. First, should the family spend part of its precious food budget on others? Second, what about appearances? Was it shameful to invite people over when the budget wouldn't stretch to buy a roast? Once again, the experts encouraged ingenuity. Modest first courses and artistically arranged salads looked elegant and took the edge off appetites. An inexpensive haddock (fish prices were generally low) could be baked and stuffed and presented at the table looking as grand as a roast.

———

The Browns casually referred to country French cooking as an inspiration for their recipes, especially those using kidneys, hearts, and other innards. But for the most part, even as they scrambled for ideas, cooking advisers in print and on the radio stuck to recognizable American food, like that haddock, and simple flavors uncomplicated by herbs and spices. A popular southern cook book proposed pouring tomato juice over leftover macaroni and cheese and stewing it with a little onion and salt for a dish brightly described as "Italian."[29] Home economics teachers in schools and social workers visiting the households of immigrant families strove to teach "American" cooking and did not try to conceal their suspicion of the food ideas people brought from the "old country"—spaghetti and meatballs, goulash, potato latkes, or the steaming blend of cabbage and potatoes the Irish called colcannon. The home economists disapproved of combining foods in one pot, of using herbs and spices, of "rich" foods and desserts. Their goal was assimilation. Luckily, they were not entirely successful. Somehow ethnic cooking traditions were transmitted and people remembered at least the taste and smell of a grandmother's cooking.

African American cooking survived, handed down verbally from generation to generation. It survived in print as well, though usually not identified by its ethnic origins. In "southern" (white middle-class) cookbooks the influence of African food was strong but unacknowledged. Robert Hall's research has shown the many foods from peanuts to yams that came to North America with Africans brought as slaves. Karen Hess, in *The Carolina Rice Kitchen*, points out, "Wherever African Americans did the cooking, there were subtle African influences even when they followed the receipts read aloud by their English mistresses. . . . It was this African presence that accounted for the near mythic reputation of Southern cooking. . . . in the South Carolina rice kitchen it was the African cook, not the mistress, who was the teacher."[30]

As writers about cooking addressed women, giving their versions of the "stone soup" recipe, they sent different messages. On the one hand, Allen never offended the sponsors of her radio program or the advertisers in the newspapers where her column appeared. She suggested ways of getting through a difficult, but temporary, situation and of keeping up appearances. But, in effect, she reinforced the misapprehension from which many women, and their husbands, suffered—that somehow they were to blame for their straitened circumstances, that it was a disgrace to be poor and out of work. The Browns, on the other hand, were on the political left; they preached resistance and encouraged their readers to politicize their response to the times. In their view, the system and the corporations were to blame, not the men whose jobs had been erased, and not their families.

Whether the cookbooks and magazines presented the message as duty to family or resistance to the pressures of a consumer society, women had to put meals on the table. What did it feel like to perform the feats required to keep a family well fed and comforted in such times? Surely there were moments when the creative foray to the butcher, the struggle with innards, and the concocting of soup grew exhausting. When the family turned up its collective nose at the dinner, when the children whined for hamburgers, the whole effort to keep from slipping—or to keep from acknowledging slipping—must often have seemed impossible. The resolute brightness of the families described in "How America Lives" probably sometimes infuriated *Ladies' Home Journal* readers.

But married women did not lose their sense of being needed. Their lives may not have been the ones they had planned, but they were neither helpless nor passive. This job, unpaid though it was, was not lost. The skills of feeding a family on little money were skills some poor people had always known; authors like Allen and the Browns transmitted them to middle-class women newly confronted with hard times. These recruits learned to shop carefully, improvise, make use of every edible crumb or leaf, adapt recipes to cut the cost by omitting an egg or using less fat and sugar, substitute bean soup for meat. These women not only helped their families to feel well fed and secure, but also raised children who actually grew up healthier than those of the previous generation. (Fitness of young men enlisting for the armed services in World War II compared favorably with those of World War I.) They knew more about nutrition than their mothers had and in a time when nothing must be wasted they saw to it that their children ate their spinach. Caroline Bird, in *The Invisible Scar*, her 1966 study of the Depression era, observes, "Even when there was not a cent in the house [these women] had an occupation. They were still in command of 'their' homes."[31]

In the emergency of the Depression, women, rebuffed by the job market, were pressed to turn their attention inward to the family circle, making a career not only of thrift and creative use of available resources, but also of attending to the psychological well-being of anxious husbands and the protection of children from the harsh realities of hard times. Contriving to put comforting meals on the table, to add treats like apple pie that cheered up the family, they warded off the fear and insecurity that lay outside their doors. Few may have recognized their work as having national significance; it was just what they could do for their families.

CHAPTER FIVE

The War in the Kitchen

WHEN THE NATION WENT TO WAR, THE RHETORIC CHANGED. THE INWARD-TURNING CONCERN FOR FAMILY THAT HAD marked the Depression years was replaced with a call to enlist in a great national effort. The command of the kitchen became a part of the campaign to win the war.

We hear a lot about Rosie the Riveter. There's even a documentary film about her. We know that more than six million women entered the labor force during World War II, nearly half in "Rosie the Riveter" factory jobs, many others in clerical work and elsewhere, "filling in" for men who had gone to war. Seventy-five percent of the women who took wartime jobs were married and most of them were mothers. But nobody filled in for them. Whether a woman took a war job, continued with her permanent work, or went on as a homemaker, the work she did at home didn't go away during the war. There were few complaints, but feeding a family became more complicated.

To make kitchen work not just an everyday necessity, but a patriotic duty, an integral part of the war effort, the United States government and the media wrapped the job in the language of the battlefield. Military imagery made home cooking part of meeting the challenge of war, summoning women to play a special role in the war effort. "Mother, captain of the kitchen, guards the health and strength of the family these difficult days," wrote Louisa Pryor Skilton in *American Cookery* magazine in March 1943. "Every American housewife . . . is all out for victory on her own home front," said Harriet H. Hesler, introducing her *300 Sugar Saving Recipes.*[1] "Kitchen Commandos" found themselves deluged with recipes with names like Victory Medley and Military Meat Balls. The slogan, "Food is a Weapon of War," appeared everywhere.

As the nation went to war, civilian life changed rapidly. The events recorded at Portsmouth, New Hampshire, by Louise Grant are typical of many cities. On December 9, 1941, two days after Pearl Harbor, the air-raid warning sounded for the first time in Portsmouth. Grant, an elementary-school teacher, and her students spent an hour in the school basement learning what to do if there should be an air raid. At home, where Grant lived with her parents, a neighbor "rang our bell & told Ma to stay in & fill the tub with water." A few days later, Grant began taking a course in first aid. She and her mother made blackout curtains for the windows and cut blue cellophane dimmers for their flashlights. Her father went to an air-raid wardens' meeting. They filled buckets with sand and put shovels next to them in case bombs should cause fires.[2]

The Japanese teacups and saucers the Grants had proudly displayed on the sideboard in the dining room "went into exile." The family bought its first war bonds. Grant went shopping for new rubber boots, and, anticipating shortages, she and her mother ordered new shoes. They decided to replace their old radio; when the new one came, "Pa got London & Buenos Aires on short wave, & that made him happy."[3]

There was a flurry of minor activity and a major wave of rumor. At the grocery store, "The store manager told Ma tea was going to be scarce," but Christmas preparations went as usual. The Grants roasted turkey and made maple nut squares and stewed apricots; mother and daughter baked sugar cookies and made chocolate ice cream. On New Year's Eve, they cooked a pork shoulder.[4]

The Grants and their Portsmouth neighbors took first-aid courses. Grant patrolled their street during blackouts and there were more air-raid drills at school. An atmosphere of emergency and preparation for anticipated further attacks prevailed in the immediate aftermath of Pearl Harbor, but the sense of imminent danger dimmed. Even in vulnerable coastal towns like Portsmouth, where watchers on shore sometimes heard—or thought they heard—the diesel engines of German submarines, the war became, for civilian Americans, a distant war of the imagination.[5]

Government had moved into the kitchen. Shortages, blackouts, and rationing provided minor frustrations on a daily basis. Programs to conserve fuel, tin, and rubber for the war effort and to divert food supplies to American armed forces and allies swung into action in the early months of war. All them affected the kitchen. Complaints were met with the endlessly reiterated, "Don't you know there's a war on?" Government officials urged conservation of resources and tried to discourage the hoarding of coffee, canned food, and other items, which began when the United States entered the war. When that didn't work, the government imposed food rationing, beginning in 1942 with sugar, and strictly controlled prices.

The Office of Price Administration (OPA) was established in 1941 to develop plans for imposing price ceilings and rationing consumer goods. In January 1942 the OPA was authorized to ration goods and regulate prices. It operated through ninety-three district offices and through local volunteer citizen rationing boards composed of individuals selected for their influence in the community. Americans initially resisted both price ceilings and rationing as undue government interference, but government propaganda persuaded them of the need for both. After some experience of standing in line for scarce goods citizens came to appreciate and support rationing as a way of distributing supplies fairly.

Uniform coupon rationing covered some items like sugar and coffee, ensuring that everyone got an equal share of scarce items. Most foods, however, were covered by point rationing. Early in 1943, each individual man, woman, or child received a ration book with red and blue stamps in point denominations of eight, five, two, and one. Red stamps could be used for meat, butter, margarine, canned fish, cheese, canned milk, fats, and oils; blue stamps were for most canned and bottled foods. This allowed people to use their stamps as they wished and choose their purchases according to taste and preference. Schools were used as centers for stamp distribution and teachers like Louise Grant dispensed them. Women, who did most of the shopping, usually controlled the ration books for the household and kept track of the complicated schedule of validation and expiration dates. (the *Portsmouth Herald*, like many other newspapers, ran a weekly "Ration Reminder" column to help them.)[6]

So committed were most women to supporting, on their metaphorical battle stations, the war that was real indeed, they almost welcomed the inconveniences and restrictions. Seldom questioning its absurdities, they seem to have accepted the huge propaganda campaign built around the metaphor of the home front, designed to foster the sense of participation among civilians far from the battlefield. Americans at home were told that every civilian act contributed to or detracted from the war effort. Standing on the home front, the kitchen soldier might consider herself a partner of the fighting men in Europe and Asia. Provided she did not look too closely at the comparatively easy time she and other Americans were having, she could see herself in league with civilians in Britain and Russia.

The woman who cooked for the family, having enlisted to fight the war in the kitchen, found herself abruptly changing of focus. Stretching meat became more important than stretching budgets. When the nation went to war, there suddenly were lots more jobs. War jobs meant money to spend. After the lean years of the Great Depression, people could finally afford to buy meat, but, to their frustration, they found that the demand outran the supply. As ingredients and equipment became scarce, housekeeping grew more complicated and more time consuming.

At the same time, women who had been told to stay home in the 1930s were pressured to take jobs in war production or to replace men who had gone to war. Volunteer work—from knitting scarves for soldiers to serving on local price control boards—demanded women's time. Already responsible for keeping up the family's health, strength, and morale, in wartime women learned that they were also in charge of conserving the national food supply, saving and recycling used fats, and managing without commercially canned foods.

Government agencies—from the long-existing Cooperative Extension Service to the new Office of Price Administration and Office of War Information (OWI)—invaded the privacy of the kitchen. They issued quantities of advice, recommendations, and rules. The men in Washington made pronouncements—sometimes avuncular, sometimes stern—emphasizing the need to supply food both to American servicemen and to our allies, especially in heavily bombed Britain.

Other, less picturesque goals were at least as important. Seeking to avoid wartime inflation, the government urged people not to spend their suddenly abundant money, but to invest their war-job earnings in war bonds. To conserve metal for war supplies, commercial canning had to be reduced to a minimum. The shortage of rubber for tires required cutting back on transportation of freight—including food stuffs—as well as on personal automobile travel.

In a full-page advertisement published in popular magazines the actress Helen Hayes, wearing a spotless little apron, is shown in her kitchen in Nyack, New York, demonstrating for two beaming visiting sailors how she strains used kitchen fat into a can to turn it in to her meat dealer. "I don't know as much about making explosives as most soldiers and sailors do about the stage," Hayes was saying coyly, "but lately I've learned these things: that kitchen fats make glycerine, and glycerine makes the powder charge that drives millions of shells from the guns of the United Nations."[7] Saving fat was one of the housewife's new jobs. "Take it to your meat dealer," the actress tells readers, "after you've collected a pound or more. He is cooperating patriotically, and will pay you for your fats and start them on their way to the war." The OPA authorized butchers to pay four cents and two meat-ration stamps for each pound. Countless coffee cans were filled with drippings and turned in to be reused in the manufacture of munitions; in the Grants' New Hampshire, women turned in 71,741 pounds of fat, enough to supply glycerine for 215,223 antiaircraft shells.[8]

There was always plenty to eat in the United States. Indeed, the government often had the embarrassment of surpluses of supposedly scarce foods, while collections of certain metals outstripped the need. But fluctuating supplies combined with transportation pressures and shortages of packaging materials required the cook constantly to re-think menus and guard against scarcity. Cooperative Extension Service staff members traveled in rural areas giving local demonstrations of canning and preserving techniques; they organized community victory gardens and distributed food bulletins; they taught sewing classes in refashioning men's and women's garments into clothes for children. They backed up these practical lessons with slide lectures on the role of food in winning the war.

To meet national goals, women were exhorted to alter their habits in the kitchen. "It is possible, of course, to sharply reduce the basic standard of living without actually impairing health, as has been demonstrated in England where the shortage of consumers' goods is acute," said a report issued by the Heller Committee for Research in Social Economics at the University of California, Berkeley. But observing the unrelenting American urge to consume, the report recognized that as late as 1944 "such a depressed level of living has not yet been accepted by the population of this country as a necessary wartime sacrifice."[9]

The home cook's challenge was to find substitutes and stretchers and to prepare them in ways that her family would accept—contriving "stick-to-the ribs" main dishes with little or no meat and comforting desserts without sugar. *The Joy of Cooking*'s 1942 edition had gone to press too soon to take rationing and shortages into consideration. To remedy the situation the publisher produced another in 1943, with a dose of wartime advice tucked in between "Table Settings" and "Menus." "The ability to adjust oneself and one's needs to an altered condition is a valuable asset," Irma Rombauer wrote with her customary pragmatism. "The conviction that the present adjustment is necessary and, if properly met, temporary, makes the adventure both interesting and thrilling. Above all, let us be cheerful about it." A few new dessert recipes sweetened with honey or corn syrup were accompanied by a list of sugar-saving recipes already in other parts of the book. Meat stretching, Rombauer pointed out, was nothing new; she drew attention to the numerous economical meat dishes and protein-rich meatless dishes long present in the book. She added some new recipes using soy beans.[10]

Even before meat rationing began, the government called for a voluntary "meatless day" each week; suggestions for meatless and low-meat dishes and meat substitutes appeared everywhere. An Agriculture Department official explained the scarcity in the pages of *Woman's Day:* more Americans were working than during the Great Depression, and with more money to spend they wanted to buy meat; American soldiers must have their meat; and the United States was shipping meat to Britain and Russia.[11] By the winter of 1942 Grant complained, "Everything is so muddled. No meat only a few fowls & some minced ham & hot dogs. No fish in the First National." Portsmouth was a fishing town, but fuel shortages and the possibility of German submarines off shore inhibited the boats from going out. Some towns fared better: the protected harbor and Cape Cod Bay allowed fishing to continue in Wellfleet, Massachusetts.[12]

Americans were not in the habit of doing without meat. In the 1927 edition of *The Boston Cooking-School Cookbook*, only one main dish featured dried beans—the familiar Boston Baked Beans. Other non-meat dishes—vegetable timbales, dainty egg dishes, and cheese rarebit—were clearly intended for ladies' luncheons and evening suppers, not for the main meal of the day. No matter how vigorously Depression-era cookbooks like the Browns' *Most for Your Money Cookbook* had urged the use of a wider variety of cuts for economy's sake, many people balked at the mere idea of eating liver, kidneys, pigs' feet, or other unfamiliar meats.

No more auspicious moment could have existed for a triumph of vegetarianism, but widespread enthusiasm for that change had to wait for a generation. The only meatless dish based on pasta that appeared with any frequency was macaroni and cheese, and vegetarian dishes of any kind were few and presented apologetically. Dull food was to be flavored with patriotic spirit. Herbs and spices were still foreign to most Americans, and few recipes took advantage of them to liven up the taste. A 1942 Helen Hokinson cartoon in *The New Yorker* showed her well-known garden club ladies seated at a table beginning their luncheon; the hostess says, "If everything has a funny taste, don't worry. It's just herbs."[13]

To make a little meat go further, wartime recipes added oatmeal or cornmeal to meat loaf mixtures, creating more bulk, if not more flavor. The accepted fact had been reiterated for decades: men like meat. *Woman's Day* of November 1942 printed a group of recipes that stretched a half pound of meat to serve four people: baked lima beans with sauerkraut and pork, sausage scrapple with peanut butter gravy (peanut butter was a popular protein additive), spaghetti with frankfurters, hamburger stew with barley and vegetables, and liver balls with noodles and a sauce made of condensed vegetable soup. The tins of spiced pork products that became famous as Spam were objects of battlefield and home front loathing. Spam, to this day, is a symbol for unappetizing wartime food, served to the troops and at home, where unconvincing efforts to make it more acceptable included treating it as a tiny ham, coated in brown sugar and dotted with cloves.

When *Woman's Day* invited its readers to submit favorite meat-less recipes, the contest winners included Fried Cheese Squares (strips of cheese dipped in an egg and flour batter and fried in drippings) and Green Pepper and Cheese Patties. These dispiriting offerings gave an impression of valiant effort but little experience of cooking without meat. Even though Wisconsin dairies were diversifying to supply equivalents of European cheeses like Roquefort, which the war had made unavailable, nearly all the wartime cheese recipes called for processed American cheese.

The sharp cutback in commercial canning made unavailable such standard ready-made main dishes as baked beans and Chef Boy-ar-dee spaghetti with tomato sauce. Some women rediscovered—whether they liked it or not—making spaghetti sauce from scratch. A wartime cookbook, in a section headed "If It Must Be—Beans!" gave recipes for Chili Con Carne made with soybeans and "Baked Beans, U.S.N." made with pork tails or feet instead of the traditional salt pork.[14] Dehydrated soups replaced scarce canned soups as lunch and supper dishes, sauces, and dips.

The scarcity of butter was hard for Americans to bear. The king in the well-known prewar A. A. Milne poem might have been a wartime complainer:

> *"Nobody,*
> *My dear,*
> *Could call me*

A fussy man,
But
I do like a little bit of butter to my bread!"

The answer, which pleased him not at all, came back:

"Many people nowadays
Like marmalade
Instead."[15]

Now he didn't even have his marmalade. In 1942, when butter was scarce and then rationed, there was not enough sugar to make marmalade. American ingenuity focused, instead, on stretching butter—making it go further by mixing it in various proportions with margarine, evaporated milk, and gelatin.

Margarine had been manufactured in the United States since 1881. Naturally chalky white and unappetizing-looking, it was subject to a 10 percent federal tax if colored to look like butter. (The butter lobby was powerful; even though Eleanor Roosevelt campaigned for repeal of this law, it was not until 1950 that restrictions on coloring margarine were lifted.) Enclosed in each package of margarine was an orange capsule of vegetable coloring. Mashing it to color the spread was a job often assigned to children, as many who were growing up during the war remember. The poet Audre Lorde recalled the sensation years later in an essay entitled "Uses of the Erotic":

> We would leave the margarine out for a while to soften, and then we would pinch the little pellet to break it inside the bag, releasing the rich yellowness into the soft pale mass of margarine. Then taking it carefully between our fingers, we would knead it gently back and forth over and over, until the color had spread through the whole pound bag of margarine.[16]

Dessert, as Ida Bailey Allen knew in the 1930s, has a substantial reputation as a morale builder. Poverty had limited dessert making during the Depression, now sugar and butter rationing again forced determined dessert makers to be inventive. They devised creations that combined oatmeal and prunes or bread crumbs and figs and explored alternative sweeteners, such as honey in lemon-prune pie or molasses in raisin pie. To celebrate her parents' forty-sixth wedding anniversary, Louise Grant managed to produce a cake using only a half cup of sugar.[17]

In order to make their households more self-sufficient than they had been for decades, many women turned back to almost-forgotten methods of home production of food, learning anew skills their grandmothers might have known. Margaret and Henry Rudkin were New Yorkers who had chosen to live a country life in Connecticut while he commuted to Wall Street on the railroad club car. Margaret Rudkin's genius for putting old skills to work has become legendary; she learned to bake in order to provide wholesome bread for her children, and by 1937 she had begun selling her homemade Pepperidge Farm bread, sending it with her husband on the morning train to Charles and Company, the purveyor of fancy food in New York. She was on her way to fame and increased fortune.

During the war, the Rudkins put the beautiful farm that had been a hobby back to real work. Margaret Rudkin wrote to the Department of Agriculture for pamphlets about raising and butchering pigs and steers and studied them. The Rudkins raised the animals and, once the butcher hired to do the slaughtering had finished his job, they cured their own meat and made lard and sausage. They stored it all in a freezer room for which they installed refrigerating machinery. "It really was very little trouble, and the quality of the meat was excellent," she recalled. Rudkin also made her own butter during the war, again following the instructions in a United States government pamphlet. Hers was one of several ingenious substitutes for whipped cream; it was made of dried milk, ice water, and lemon juice.[18]

The Rudkins had plenty of space and money and so they were able to deal with wartime shortages by becoming self-sufficient producers for the duration. Humbler souls did what they could to grow and preserve their own vegetables and fruits. Where space was limited and backyards didn't exist, community gardens occupied empty lots and corners. Encouraged by the government, Americans planted twenty million victory gardens by the fall of 1943 and raised 40 percent of their vegetables.[19] In Portsmouth, Grant and her parents sent away for seeds and started tomatoes, peppers, beets, carrots, lettuce, and other vegetables. The vegetable garden eventually spread from the backyard to occupy the whole front yard as well. It took up much of Grant's time, from starting seeds indoors in late winter to setting out plants in spring, weeding and watering in summer, and harvesting and preserving the crops in late summer and fall.

Not every American family grew its own food, but someone in every family shopped. Women soon found that they had to devote more time to this chore. Instead of going to one grocery or supermarket, they shopped from store to store to get what they wanted. They stood in line for a share of a grocer's shipment of sugar or coffee; they hunted (sometimes unsuccessfully) for a turkey for Thanksgiving or Christmas; they used their favored-customer status at the local grocery and shopped the supermarkets as well.

Gas rationing, combined with unpredictable food shortages, made shopping more complicated. Local boards determined how gas was allocated; most families had "A" stickers, allowing them the minimum. Grant walked downtown to meet her mother after school, and together they did the shopping on foot: "Only way we can get our heavy bundles home with this nuisance of a gas situation." Some shortages of familiar "basics"—sugar, butter, meat—lasted for the duration or longer. Others were less predictable. Grant, like Americans across the country, found herself buying a half pound of coffee— she had never before bought less than a pound—on September 30, 1942; two and a half weeks later, she stood in line for another half pound. A few days after that, she heard the sound of the coffee grinder as she was shopping in the A & P and, moving quickly, acquired another half pound.[20] As if in pursuit of such persevering shoppers, the government announced coffee rationing shortly thereafter.

In case anyone hadn't heard, there was a war on. The government gave it full voice. Magazines, newspapers, and radio programs kept audiences informed about restrictions and availability of food. A government-sponsored radio show featured "Aunt Sammy" offering cooking tips. Advice was plentiful. *Woman's Day* added a special section, with a last-minute deadline, for current information on shortages and substitutes. Government officials at OPA and the Department of Agriculture (USDA) published articles explaining why shortages of particular foods occurred, how the ration point system worked, and why wage and price freezes were put into effect.

In the fall of 1943, Roy F. Hendrickson of the Department of Agriculture told a story in the columns of *Woman's Day*. "A bunch of us men," he said, had met to try to figure out how they could persuade women to shift their thinking to meet sudden changes in the food supply. There was one woman at the meeting. Apparently the men hadn't expected her to speak; they were surprised, by Hendrickson's account, when she "interrupted." But she was exasperated by their apprehensions: "She pooh-poohed our fears. Why, she said, fling a challenge to a woman and just watch her take it." This anonymous female adviser (he never mentions her name) recommended radio. "'Women will listen to the radio for news on foods,' she told us, 'the way intelligence officers in the army listen to short-wave broadcasts.'" Her recommendation: "Give it to them straight and they will take it."[21]

The radio had been women's companion in the kitchen for many years, and homemaking programs occupied many daytime hours. The men of the USDA were convinced. Soon Billie Burke—still famous today as the blonde, bubbly Good Witch in *The Wizard of Oz*—was playing a point-perplexed housewife on a weekly radio program called "Fashions in Rations." In her high-pitched, girlish voice, she queried her guests, authorities from government and industry, who explained the latest changes in food rationing and availability. Elsewhere, local cooking programs that had been around for years shifted their emphasis. Jessie Young, the "radio homemaker" of Iowa radio station KMA, broadcasting from her own kitchen, devised wartime recipes like Marbled Macaroni (with tomato sauce, American cheese, and Spam), a loaf called "Yakima Meatless" made of ground kidney beans, cottage cheese, and soda crackers, and Mock Hamburgers made of oatmeal and eggs flavored with onions and sage, cooked in tomato juice.[22]

The aggressive marketing of the 1920s had taught people to appreciate the convenience of commercially processed foods. Americans had learned to take for granted canned and frozen vegetables and fruits, already trimmed and cut, barely in need of cooking, and available all year round. Now, out of duty, not pleasure, they were required to reacquaint themselves with cooking and eating fresh locally grown produce in season. "We'll search for quick easy methods of preparing fresh vegetables because we will have to eat more fresh foods," wrote food expert Cora Anthony in March 1943.[23] Her plain-Jane suggestions included kale with potatoes, baked vegetable hash, and scallions, peas and cabbage served with an egg.

"The soybean, long in use in the Orient, is being given a tardy national recognition," declared Rombauer in the wartime edition of *The Joy of Cooking*. "It is even rumored that it will make the social grade, so be prepared to meet it shortly, with the proper patriotic enthusiasm, in the best of houses." Rombauer's authority among housewives was hard to match, but the government issued official pronouncements urging people who very likely had never heard of such things to eat soybeans, use soy flour, and grow their own bean sprouts. The official literature encouraged Americans to use soybeans to beat the food shortages and defeat Hitler. Soybeans "really need an uplift, being rather on the dull side," Rombauer admitted, "but (like some of our friends) respond readily to the right contacts."[24] And she suggested some relatively sprightly ways to dress them up for the dinner table. But official public relations efforts and even Rombauer's recipes were not enough to overcome the blandness of the basic ingredient. More imaginative uses of soy and soy products such as tofu would not appear until the vegetarian movement of the sixties and seventies. Meanwhile, the spirit of sacrifice for country, it appeared, was not to show itself in cooking savory casseroles.

The meat ration allowance was generous (two and a half pounds per person per week seems high by today's standards) but stores simply did not have enough of the steaks and roasts Americans were accustomed to. To compensate for what was perceived as great scarcity, meat eaters were driven to explore less familiar cuts—spareribs, pork tails, oxtails, and innards—which bore the stigma of being poor people's food. Some tried horsemeat—but seldom more than once. In February 1943, Grant triumphantly noted in her diary, "Got a piece of corned beef!" and remarked wistfully, "How I would like a little smoked shoulder or ham."[25] The recipes for tougher, bonier meats were similar to those of Depression-era cookbooks. The motivational message that accompanied them was no longer thrift, but patriotism.

Nothing must go to waste. Housekeeping advice has always regarded waste as a major sin, but now the reason not to transgress was concern for those distant others—fighting men and their battlefield allies—rather than for a domestic budget. "You haven't saved it until you've used it," chided *Woman's Day* in May 1945, introducing a chart showing how to use leftovers.

Government officials turned to homemakers to use up surplus crops, sometimes grown with excessive encouragement from the government. "It is up to you and me to eat the things that the farmers grow for us," a Department of Agriculture representative preached in the pages of a popular magazine, "even if it means eating the same food several days in a row." In 1943, a billion-pound peanut crop far exceeded the demand for peanut butter sandwiches, which accounts for the sometimes bizarre inclusion of peanut butter in bean casseroles and in sauces (Asian cooking was unknown beyond chop suey to most Americans). When farmers grew too many sweet potatoes, women were expected to find ways to use them. Never mind if a family, dutifully following government advice, had grown a good crop of white potatoes in the victory garden; save them for later, the voice of government warned, for we must keep the farmers happy. "There's a long winter ahead and it may be a hard one. There is a war to win, and it may be a long one."[26]

While some felt a sense of patriotic virtue in consuming bland meatless meals, not everybody signed on for austerity. "Bluntly speaking," announced the president of the Gourmet Society in New York in the fall of 1941, "it is exceedingly important to our total happiness that we enjoy our dinner."[27] And in a 1943 cookbook called *Cooking on a Ration*, the author, Marjorie Mills, reminded readers, "In this troubled universe it's more than ever important to make mealtime loom up as a little island of serenity and contentment."[28]

Whatever serenity was wrought was accomplished by the efforts of women in their kitchens. Women who had never confronted a stove (nearly half of all upper-middle-class households before the war had household help) had to juggle changing regulations and shortages at the same time that they were just plain learning to cook. And, in some cases, to can. By the summer of 1942, *Woman's Day* published an article on methods of preserving food at home. While metal for commercial canning was scarce, the supply of glass jars, rubber rings, and lids seemed adequate for the time being (later it would become a problem). The article explained techniques of hot-water-bath and pressure-cooker canning. It also described other methods of food preservation. Cold storage—in basements, storage banks or pits, and outdoor root cellars—was a method that most rural people a generation earlier would have been familiar with. Drying vegetables at home was a simple way to keep parsley, celery, and onions. A more esoteric idea was cooking tomato paste until thick, then drying it a half-inch thick in a shallow pan and cutting it in pieces for storage. Among techniques of the past that were revived were salting fish and making sauerkraut. One couple living through the war years at the far end of Cape Cod tried salting green beans in a barrel. The result was disastrous: the beans turned a grim shade of gray and "tasted dreadful."[29]

Pressure cookers, the safest equipment for home canning, were in short supply. People who were lucky enough to own one were urged to share it. Communities organized canning centers where women could share equipment and beginners could learn techniques. Such centers became the scene of convivial gatherings not unlike the old quilting bees.

Martha Garland, a Cooperative Extension Service agent in New Hampshire, traveled to twenty-seven communities in the summer of 1942 to help them set up canning groups. She sent out a follow-up questionnaire in September. The 212 participants who responded (about half the total) had put up 39,874 quarts of food. A woman in Danville, New Hampshire, wrote simply, "Canned everything in sight."[30] That summer, Louise Grant and her mother laid in a supply of jars for canning. In September and October they put up sixty-one quarts of tomatoes from their garden. They also made mincemeat and piccalilli. The Grants augmented the produce of their own garden by buying additional produce—wax beans and peas—from nearby farmers, which they also canned. And they exchanged fruits and vegetables with friends.

The next year, Grant recorded that they had put up 299 jars of "stuff"—tomatoes, beans, peas, carrots, pears, applesauce, as well as ketchup, relishes, chili sauce, and jam. By the fall of 1943, jars were hard to come by. Grant describes bottling their homemade ketchup in "an odd asst of bottles—1 pt Coldwells' rum with a ship pressed in—1 pt M1-31, a Hubbards germicide bottle, a pepper sauce bottle, an olive jar, & a candy jar."[31]

Although the food supply was always adequate, America restructured its cooking and eating habits. In fact, as it turned out, Americans, forced to eat less fat, meat, and sugar and more fresh vegetables, unwittingly ate a more nutritious diet and were healthier during the war years than ever before. Rich and poor had similarly nutritious food, though the rich might have chops and asparagus while the poor ate meat loaf and spinach.

The National Nutrition Conference for Defense, called by President Roosevelt in the spring of 1941—before Pearl Harbor—had established standards for a healthy diet in the form of seven "food groups." The conference report recommended one pint of milk daily for adults, and one quart for children over the age of two; one serving of meat, one egg or a substitute such as beans; two servings of vegetables, one of them green or yellow; two servings of fruit, including one good source of vitamin C such as oranges or grapefruits; whole grain or enriched bread, flour, or cereal, butter or margarine, and dessert at least once a day. But the recommendations, which don't look surprising from today's perspective, pointed the way toward more sophisticated, more nutritious eating for a meat-and-potatoes nation.

The nutrition message was delivered as widely as possible and the campaign, along with wartime prosperity, worked. At school, children sang songs that emphasized the importance of milk, vegetables, and protein. Borrowing the tune from "The Battle Hymn of the Republic," one such song, "Food—a Weapon of Our Nation," dedicated a verse (in forced rhyme and bumpy rhythm) to lunch-box nutrition:

> *In the lunch box you must put a hot and creamy soup, not tea,*
> *Make the sandwiches of whole wheat bread with meatloaf, cheese,*
>   *poultry,*

You must sometimes add an egg and always fruit or celery
In all our factories,

(Chorus)
    Pack a lunch a man can work on
    Pack a lunch a man can work on
    Pack a lunch a man can work on
    In all our factories.[32]

Presumably the children went home to exhort their mothers with this chorus. Women made box lunches, not only for children, but also for husbands and other members of their families (sometimes including themselves) who worked factory shifts. Factories allowed as little as fifteen minutes for lunch, often not enough time to get to the cafeteria. Some had no cafeteria. Some people worked too far away to waste precious gasoline coming home for midday dinner.

The magazines, like the song, urged ample lunches. They encouraged efficient production. They advised establishing an area of the kitchen where lunch boxes were packed and planning ahead. In "Victory Lunches: Hearty Food for Sturdy Men," Skilton proposed a community effort. "Why not take turns packing these Victory lunches? It is no more trouble to plan for two, four or six men, and by taking turn and turn about, it would certainly lighten the work."[33]

Husbands relied on wives to provide individual lunches, but women workers sometimes extended the pot luck principle to the factory—they brought food to share. Some, providing the ethnic dishes that were traditional in their families, brightened the night shift and broadened their fellow workers' tastes.[34]

By late 1944, patriotism in the kitchen had become tiresome to many. Selfishness was gaining on the sense of common purpose. A chorus of complaints arose when there were not enough turkeys to go around for the holidays; many people did not enjoy settling for pork, veal shoulder, or braised fowl. In New Hampshire, the Grants were lucky to have a turkey for Thanksgiving but on December 21, with "no birds in view," they settled on a stewing hen and a smoked shoulder for Christmas dinner. Dried apricots were so scarce that finding some merited a triumphant comment in Grant's diary. Canned grapefruit and orange juice were rationed again. Like most Americans, the Grants listened faithfully to the evening news. When commentator Gabriel Heatter announced that shortening would return to the ration list, Louise made a hasty trip to the store before closing time to stock up. Her early noncritical willingness to cooperate was yielding to cynicism; she scornfully renamed the OPA the Office of Perfidious Administration.[35]

By summer, the Grants considered themselves lucky to get a piece of meat at all, even when it took two trips to the store. One Saturday morning, Louise Grant and her mother went shopping but had "No luck for food." Louise walked back in the afternoon and "stood & stood & was lucky. Got a nice piece of ham." Two weeks later she left off shelling peas to get to the store early, only to find the butcher expected a delivery in the afternoon. She returned and "Stood from quarter of 2 until 3 but got some," then returned to shelling and canning twenty-three pints of peas, making soup, and cooking the hard-won piece of lamb.[36]

Patriotic rhetoric firmly defined wartime cooking as a response to an emergency. "Doing without," like women's work in factories, was a way of supporting the boys at the front and licking Hitler and Hirohito. When the war was over, the "boys" came back hungry, and they didn't want Spam. Most of the women (though not always willingly) left their jobs and went back to full time homemaking. Wartime recipes were gleefully discarded along with blackout shades and rayon stockings.

The advertising industry, with few products to sell during the war, had turned its talents to delivering the government's messages of patriotism and the war effort. Manufacturers whose production line had switched over to delivering weapons and K-rations kept their names before the public with patriotic ads. But well before the war ended, the magazine pages filled with ads designed to whet appetites for the new refrigerators that would be women's reward for winning the war—in the kitchen.

With V-E and V-J days celebrated, the lunch boxes and canning equipment were discarded. The shortages ended, though not immediately or all at once. Good red meat returned to the dinner table. It would be twenty-five years before serious vegetarian cooking commanded any sizable audience, and by then the postwar enthusiasm for ethnic cooking would have changed American attitudes about herbs and spices and cooking with wine.

The war in the kitchen was over. Abundant good food for all was one of the things the country had fought to preserve. After all, one of President Roosevelt's Four Freedoms was Freedom from Want. In the Norman Rockwell illustration, a comfortable, motherly woman in an apron sets before the family a magnificent, enormous, well-browned, luscious turkey surrounded by platters and bowls of buttered vegetables, mashed potatoes, rolls, and well-sugared cranberry sauce, which is sure to be followed by apple pie.

This traditional image of the mature woman as provider of plenty had been taken for granted before the war. It was set aside for the duration, and the official image that replaced it gave women at home and in wartime jobs a role in winning the conflict. Their unpaid efforts in the kitchen—little appreciated in peacetime—were acknowledged during the war years as important to the national interest. When the war was over, that value disappeared along with women's war jobs. The captain of the kitchen was once again just a housewife.

CHAPTER SIX

Tuna-Noodle Casserole

THE SIDEBARS OF *WOMAN'S DAY* WHISPERED OF FUTURE
PLENTY, EVEN AS THE RECIPES FOR SPAM CONTINUED TO
roll out. Inside the front covers of magazines in 1944 and 1945, dream
refrigerators and stoves gleamed in glossy color. All through the war
American women had been told that their job was to save, stretch,
reuse, make things last, contrive to get along. But the 1939 New York
World's Fair had shown them plenty of high-technology future to
dream about, and long before the war ended, advertisers were preparing for a shift back to domestic production.

The stern messages of wartime restraint began to give way to the
encouragement of peacetime desire. Wartime propaganda had made
conformity a patriotic duty, and as the nation moved from war to
peace, the advertising men seized the moment of transition. They
took this conformity and privatized it. And the target of their postwar
effort responded. Relieved of their pseudo-military roles, women
embraced new assignments as consumers. During the war they had
become accustomed to taking information and instruction through
magazines and radio. After the war, as government advice and instruction faded away, advertisers deftly moved into the empty space to sell
appliances and processed food. With sugared words and pictures, the
ads reminded the public once again that abundance is at the core of
the American dream. Consuming for its own sake, and not just to
keep body and soul together, was the rule for the postwar world.

Some aspects of wartime austerity lingered as the men came home. Sugar rationing continued for a while. In 1947, President Harry S. Truman asked Americans to observe a voluntary meatless day each week to share our plenty with people in Europe, where hunger continued and shortages and rationing were far more than simply a nuisance. But the war was over. With that one nod to generosity, Americans demanded meat. When meat producers raised prices to astronomical levels, government attempted to exert control; women refused to cooperate. They wanted meat, no matter what the price. They had followed the OPA rules through the war; now they demanded the right to pay higher prices for the meat they were determined to have.

During the Depression, people had done without things they couldn't afford, to keep the family together. During the war, they had done without things as patriotic participants helping to bring victory, while enduring separation from family members. It was time for an end to shortages and doing without.

The America that moved into the 1950s had emerged from two decades of exceptional circumstances. Before 1930, as myth would have it, America had been a prosperous and peaceful nation. Since the young couple of the 1950s hadn't been there, they were free to fantasize about the old-fashioned family living a quiet, secure life without fear—a *Saturday Evening Post*–cover version of the past. Many people looked at this picture with considerable nostalgia. The abundant food, the lavish supply of eggs and butter, the old-fashioned cooking of rural America appealed to senses craving rich tastes, and the distance in time made it easy to gloss over the past's rough edges. At the war's end, the marketers of domesticity told stories about the good old days of plenty long ago and, like the wicked gnome in a fairy tale, surrounded housewives with temptation in the form of advertisements for brand new appliances and marvelous modern kitchens, instant mashed potatoes and Reddi-Whip.

The fast-expanding suburbs of postwar America hardly resembled the rural towns where the fantasy of past times was set. American middle-class families didn't stay in the same place anymore. New households formed in the ranch houses or split-levels of new suburban communities; between 1950 and 1960 the suburban population increased nearly 50 percent. Young men went to work for large companies and when they were transferred, they moved their young families. New supermarkets appeared to meet the shopping needs of new suburbanites. In many families, the husband-father left early in the morning to commute to work in the city and came home late; the prized togetherness was restricted to weekends.

The most visible image of American life became the suburban family. In 1947 the first Levittown had opened, offering single-family houses—initially for whites only—with their own tiny yards; G. I. mortgages and low prices meant young white families could afford to own their own homes. Veterans back from the war were eager to get on with their lives, to make up for lost time; and meanwhile another cohort was coming up, mingling in colleges with the more mature G.I.–bill students and their families. Their elders were anxious to impose a safe pattern of family life on the nation's restless young people.

People who married young (often having saved sex for after the wedding) aspired to a separate house and yard of their own, however small, with a mortgage to pay and a lawn to mow. These were not likely to be rebellious members of society. A man's job in business, even if it was boring, paid the mortgage and the car payments and the grocery bill; a wife's domestic work kept the operation humming along. In the ideal family of the fifties, gender roles were clearly defined: men were breadwinners, women were homemakers. "The long-held dream of a fulfilling family life in a comfortable home seemed at last to be coming true for millions of people; not everyone was affluent or middle class, but it was assumed that those left out would eventually get their share," writes the psychologist Arlene Skolnick in *Embattled Paradise*, her study of American family life.[1]

Contrary to the usual image of the fifties, not all married women stayed home. "Despite the rhetoric and reality of domesticity," notes Skolnick, "millions of women entered the workplace during the 1950s." Middle-class married women over thirty-five accounted for much of the increase. But they did not enter with the same goals as men. In another study, Elaine Tyler May, a social historian, points out that most of these women "sought employment, ironically, to promote their role as consumers . . . . Many employed wives considered their jobs secondary to their role as consumers and in tune with the ethic of togetherness and subordination that characterized their marital relationships. . . . women sought employment to bolster the family budget but not to disrupt domestic power relationships. As long as their employment provided a secondary source of income and did not undermine the authority of the male breadwinner, it was acceptable to the family."[2]

Suburban social life centered in the immediate community, and women traded child-care hours. It might have been a time such as Melusina Fay Peirce envisioned when families living in close proximity could share equipment and services, but there was little that was communal about postwar housing developments; to each her own electric stove, to each his own lawn mower seemed to be the creed. Families turned their attention inward, seeking what they imagined to be the strength and self-sufficiency of pioneer settlers.

The fifties has become a code word for smothering domesticity. It was not, however, the domesticity of Mrs. Abney and her neighbors; it depended on manufactured goods and the supermarket. The suburbs, the supermarket, and the white middle-class woman the admen fondly called "Mrs. Consumer" existed in a triangular relationship. An old-fashioned life with modern conveniences—that was the vision for postwar America.

For young wives living far from their own families, brand names took the place of mother's advice in the kitchen. And if they needed a female role model, Betty Crocker was there. *Betty Crocker's Picture Cookbook* was on the best seller list.

Who was Betty Crocker? She was the creation of an advertising department, and she'd been around for thirty years. Like many good fictional characters, she had assumed a convincingly real presence as an omniscient and reassuring domestic adviser. This was not the same as having your own mother show you how to roll a pie crust, any more than the alarm clock and hot water bottle wrapped in a blanket to comfort a puppy are like her real mother, but the General Mills staff certainly tried, with pictures and text, to give her that role. Her radio "voice" and magazine-ad image, as well as the printed recipes, could almost convince her audience that she was as real as Fannie Farmer.

Betty Crocker's cookbook, foreshadowing the television cooking shows that began a decade later, taught cooking through step-by-step black-and-white photographs and provided inspiration through brilliant color pictures of finished products. It hewed firmly to the line of "American" cooking that the home economists had decreed in the twenties. Meat and vegetable recipes were simple, basic and unembellished, presented in the straightforward tone of essential information. Cakes and pies were a different matter. The book's biggest and most elaborate sections concerned baking—not surprising since General Mills was a major producer of flour and cake mixes. "Cakes—A Symbol of Home Life," trumpeted the chapter heading, and Betty Crocker encouraged her reader to "be a good ar-cake-techt."[3] Mothers might dream of designing ships, but they could follow instructions and make a sailboat birthday cake for a child, baking a cake mix in a square pan, cutting it on the diagonal to create a hull and two sails, and painting it realistically with white and chocolate frosting.

If cakes stood for home, pies stood for the nation. Betty Crocker's chapter title pointed the moral: "Pie—A Symbol of Good Eating in a Good Land." It seemed virtually unpatriotic not to get out the rolling pin. After all, Betty Crocker said, "Pie is as American as the Fourth of July."[4] If women suppressed desires to be architects or ship designers, perhaps they could emulate the farm women of Napton, Missouri, taking pride and pleasure—and even a patriotic glow—in building lattice-crusted pies.

Their constructions, however, were likely to be as counterfeit as a cardboard model of the Empire State Building. The pie and cake recipes so treasured and reluctantly shared by the women of Napton had been transformed into formula-made mixes by food manufacturers. Inventiveness had largely been appropriated by the people behind the imaginary Betty Crocker—forty-eight home economists in the laboratory kitchens at General Foods. All the cook had to do was add water—and sometimes eggs—and mix. For their processing plants, manufacturers demanded uniform crops from farmers. Scientists in test kitchens dreamed up new variations of their packaged foods and printed their foolproof recipes on boxes of cake mix and cans of tomatoes. The first woman in the neighborhood to try one of these recipes might gather some applause, but her creativity was hardly her own. Blueberry muffins made from a mix and the little can of stewed berries that accompanied it could be baked in miniature-sized pans for a coffee, but that hardly constituted invention and for anyone who remembered the real thing, hardly met the definition of blueberry muffins.

Appearance mattered more than how it was achieved. To inspire and aid their cooking, women of the 1950s had frozen foods, canned goods, packaged mixes—a host of products. Some of them were new: instant mashed potatoes, aerosol whipped cream, Cheese Whiz, Bisquick, and Lipton's dried onion soup (notice that it's virtually impossible to talk about the fifties without mentioning brand names). Others, like Jell-O (invented in 1897), were old-timers that achieved their crowning moment then.

Not long ago, a friend of mine from those days, now a well-traveled and sophisticated cook whose husband maintains a notable wine cellar, was vacationing with her husband and grown children at a lakeside cabin inherited from her husband's parents. She decided to treat them to a special dinner. They began with cocktails (frozen daiquiris and whiskey sours) and appetizers (clam dip and cheese logs made of Olde English and Roquefort cheese spreads mixed together and rolled into a log covered with ground nuts). The salad was wedges of iceberg lettuce with bottled Russian dressing. The main dish was a casserole—chicken and noodles, with a sauce made of canned mushroom soup and Velveeta cheese. She served frozen green beans with mushroom soup sauce, topped with canned French fried onion rings. She made aspic out of lemon Jell-O and tomato juice; it was filled with celery, sliced olives, and canned shrimp, jelled in a ring mold, and served with mayonnaise. There were brown-and-serve rolls. The wine was a jug of Almaden rosé. Dessert was a Betty Crocker specialty, Biscuit Tortoni. For this she combined macaroon crumbs, diced candied cherries, and chopped salted almonds, folded the mixture into softened vanilla ice cream, and froze it in little paper cups. Her perplexed, near-middle-aged children were well into the feast before they recognized that their mother had carried them back to the decade when they were born. For those of you who were around in the fifties, this sounds familiar. For those who weren't, it's just what you were afraid of. My friend's dinner came straight from her own and her mother-in-law's 1950s recipe file.[5]

A working man who commuted to the city by train or car every day had a right to expect to come home to a "home-cooked meal." But modern women didn't expect to slave in the kitchen all day as they imagined their grandmothers' having done. Electric appliances, processed foods, and a little ingenuity substituted for time and effort. A new synthesis of tradition and modern technology occurred. Science—the great discovery of turn-of-the-century home economists—was built into postwar kitchens along with the modular cabinets and bright Formica counters. "Kitchen-tested recipes" and standardized measurements were taken for granted.

An illustration in one of the Betty Crocker cookbooks—one of those cute little cartoonish sketches—shows a husband and wife arriving home to their sweet suburban ranch house. He's coming in the back door, in business suit and hat, carrying his briefcase; she's coming in the front door, carrying her golf clubs. The many middle-class women who worked, along with women of color and poor women, were not visible, even in such middle-class publications. Twelve million American women had jobs, but the images in cookbooks and in magazines suggested that whatever time could be saved on housework was available for having fun.

Not even higher education discouraged such a view. Earlier generations of women educated at Smith or Mount Holyoke or Oberlin or Cornell had prized their hard-won education and felt obliged to turn it to good use. They became missionaries or settlement-house workers or teachers, often renouncing marriage; they went into political reform, calling it "municipal housekeeping" to avoid alarming men. Some entered law or medicine or earned a Ph.D.; they had a long hard road. But women of the postwar years were bent on marrying, even those who did go to law school or received other graduate education. "In 1930 half of all professionals were women," writes Skolnick. "But in the 1950s, most women who attended college had no career plans, and dropped out in large numbers to marry. College was the place for a young woman to find a husband and to acquire the polish to carry off the role of the doctor's or lawyer's or organization man's gracious wife."[6] College women took for granted what earlier generations of women had prized. The number of women earning Ph.D.'s actually dropped. Students at Smith College were encouraged to go forth and raise the intellectual level of the community, not to run for office or a company. And in the fifties most did what they were told. The professional world was hardly clamoring for women; the avenues open for women were short and did not lead to the top. May cites a survey that found "close to half the men and over a third of the women agreed with the statement that it was 'unnatural' for women to be placed in positions of authority over men."[7]

Cold war anxiety exaggerated notions of strong, conventional nuclear families. The containment policies that governed international relations, May says, were mirrored by "domestic containment" at home; Americans "looked toward home as a way to bolster themselves against potential threats." Instead of building on the advances women had made in independence and career during the Depression and the war to create "a new model family with two equal partners who shared breadwinning and homemaking tasks," middle-class Americans turned inward.[8]

When my husband and I married in 1952, our friends and relatives equipped us with a blender (one speed), a pop-up toaster, an electric beater, an electric waffle iron that doubled as a sandwich grill, copper-bottomed saucepans, and several too many pepper mills—all the most up-to-date in kitchen technology. Even our rotary egg beater (an invention that dates far back into the nineteenth century) was equipped with ball bearings to make it run smoothly.

The Connecticut neighborhood where we lived was just like the one in the advertisers' minds (not surprising, since some of the ad men were our neighbors). In a subdivision that itself was less than a decade old, where the streets were named for World War II generals and admirals—Marshall, Nimitz, MacArthur—everyone was new. Those who had been there a year or two were eager to be neighborly to newcomers. Families with one salary and numerous babies had not much money for baby sitters, let alone for travel.

Nearly every family had small children, and only a handful of women held even part-time jobs. Men were responsible for supporting their families; most of them worked in New York City for a large company, an advertising agency, or a bank. They left to catch the train early in the morning, wearing Brooks Brothers suits and conservative neckties and hats—felt in winter, straw in summer. By the time they got home it was seven o'clock or so; the children had had their baths and supper. Women took charge of housekeeping, child care, meals, and everything else that came up during all the hours their husbands were away, from getting the washing machine repaired to taking a child to the emergency room for stitches.

Social life revolved around children and food. Stranded in the suburbs, women, feeling a vestigial need for some sort of communal life, made excuses to get together and talk to someone older than four. They visited in the morning or afternoon. At the slightest cause for festivity, they gave coffees for each other, baking little sweets and fancy breads to spread around an industrial-sized percolator. They were all about the same age. New recipes circulated. Most of them were clipped from magazines; few were passed down from elders. These housewives had long hours to fill between their husbands' early morning departure and their return on the 6:02 or the 7:14 train at night. As families moved in and out, following job transfers, coffee parties were gestures of welcome or farewell. Baby showers were frequent.

As dining rooms grew smaller or became (as ours was) just an ell on the living room, kitchens expanded. In a household where the cook was also the lady of the house and supervisor of the children, the kitchen became the center of family life. These rooms would have won the approval of Marie Meloney, the Better Homes in America tastemaker—they boasted efficient floor plans and modular cabinets, easy-to-clean surfaces and appliances in fashionable colors. My own ranch house kitchen, like thousands of others, had yellow Formica counter tops and a built-in table to match, washable wallpaper in a bright kitchen motif of fruits and vegetables, a vinyl floor, and a Harvest Gold refrigerator and stove, all combining efficiency and cleanliness with a resolutely cheerful decorative touch.

Small electric appliances gathered on kitchen counters or in specially designed cabinets (or lurked in back corners and were never used). Treating cooking as a laboratory science may have seemed an adventure when Fannie Farmer and others introduced level measurements to an earlier generation; housewives in the 1950s took for granted that they would measure and sift ingredients, and twirl thermostats on ovens and electric skillets to exact temperatures. They mopped and sponged and cursed the necessity of defrosting the refrigerators that grew glacial deposits of ice.

A nostalgic image of the nurturing kitchen of the past was superimposed on the sterile modern kitchen that prewar domestic science had achieved. But whereas the nineteenth-century woman in the kitchen had been a producer, and often a supervisor of at least one employee, her postwar counterpart was a consumer and alone. The productive housewife, dealing with produce and meat grown on the family farm, responsible for the whole process, providing the comfort of a home-grown food supply, was replaced in the fifties by a woman pushing a supermarket cart, bending over a freezer, or peering into a refrigerator. The work represented a marriage of domesticity and convenience, but the idea of the self-sufficient farm kitchen, with all its abundance, its pots simmering on the back of the stove, its bread rising in the oven, was crucial to the atmosphere they hoped to create.

The title of Fannie Farmer's *Boston Cooking-School Cookbook* had evoked the idea of learning skills. The book that exemplifies the prevailing approach to cooking in the fifties is called *The Can-Opener Cookbook*. In it, Poppy Cannon, a journalist, elevated that humble instrument (not yet electrified) to a major role in the home kitchen. "When I ply my busy little can opener," she wrote, "I move onto the scene the way a chef comes in after a corps of kitchen helpers has done the scullery chores—the drudgery of cooking. Armed with a can opener, I become the artist-cook, the master, the creative chef."[9]

Like most of my suburban neighbors, with my Dazey can opener secure on its wall bracket, I plunged wholeheartedly into a life of kids and casseroles. I filled the modular metal cabinets with mixes and canned goods. The refrigerator's freezer held neat packages of uniform-sized green beans and French fries, blocks of frozen fish and fish sticks (where did all those square fish swim?), pale chicken pies.

Women prided themselves on preparedness and organization, but it was based on planning and shopping, not on food production.

Home cooking in the fifties relied, not on old family recipes, but, as my friend's menu suggests, on new ones copied from cheery magazines or the backs of boxes. They were the concoctions of food manufacturers' staff home economists. Onion soup dip, three bean salad, tuna-noodle casserole, frozen spinach "creamed" with canned mushroom soup, fanciful structures based on Jell-O, cream pies made with packaged graham cracker crust and pudding mix and topped with Reddi-Whip—meals like these emerged daily from kitchens in suburbia. The houses (as Malvina Reynolds observed in her wonderful song "Little Boxes") all looked just the same, distinguished from one another by the color of the shutters. The food served in them was hardly more original. Ingenuity consisted of the clever combining of processed foods. The overall effect, it's safe to say, was uniquely American.

Tuna-noodle casserole is the emblematic dish of the postwar kitchen. No, there was not always tuna-noodle casserole—but it sometimes seems that way. It had many variations. The basic ingredients, as every American knows, are canned tuna fish, noodles or macaroni, and some kind of cream sauce. It's elegant to make your own cream sauce from butter, flour, and milk (cream sauce is one of those things that's a test of a good cook and for that very reason, it's a challenge to the less confident). The cookbooks might urge the value of learning to make a smooth cream sauce, using their exact formulas to achieve the precise thickness and richness desired, but any woman who preferred to avoid this task could open a can of soup. Science in the kitchen diminished in value when manufacturers served up recipes using a can of this, a box of that. Anyway, what could be more scientific than the commercial product, guided by a formula, prepared under carefully controlled conditions for maximum uniformity.

Manufacturers convinced a lot of people that canned concentrated mushroom soup, thinned with a little milk, was as good as, if not better than, homemade cream sauce, and the concentration was in the soup, not the cook. Canned tuna fish required no effort and, like noodles, was always there in even a minimally stocked kitchen. The dish could be topped with grated cheese or even Cheese Whiz.

Finally, in 1960, Peg Bracken, a successor to Poppy Cannon who boldly confronted the truth that some people who have to cook hate to cook, reduced tuna-noodle casserole to the utmost simplicity. In *The I-Hate-To-Cook Book,* she reveals a method that requires opening three cans. Sandwiched between the contents of two cans of macaroni and cheese is the tuna. A few minutes in the oven, *et voilà!*

Tuna-noodle casserole is one way of dealing with the daily necessity of producing dinner. It's bland enough to offend no one, not even fussy children; it's cheap and it's filling. Because it is all these things, it comes to the mind of the cook responsible for dreaming up daily menus often—too often. The curse of it is boredom.

Once, the recipes women took pride in were their own—perhaps handed down as a family favorite—a cake or bread or soup that the individual had perfected with pride. This was true in the rural Napton cookbook of 1928. But by midcentury, community cookbooks in which women share their favorite recipes all looked pretty much alike. The standard recipes were things like Coca Cola cake and three bean salad, handed down, not from great-grandmother, but from General Foods.

The food manufacturers offered all sorts of ready-made food, food that only needed to be thawed, or to have water added, or to be stuck in the oven for a while. Packages on supermarket shelves beckoned the shopper. Starting from scratch was out, but domesticity was in.

It was not enough to use these products straight. Encouraged by the clever recipes devised by food-company domestic scientists, housewives added fruit to gingerbread mix and made Welsh rarebit with canned tomato soup. One month I clipped a dozen recipes from *Woman's Day*—all featuring hot dogs in various disguises. Carrying out all these transformations and embellishments made family cooks feel clever. Though it may have been billed as a return to normalcy, 1950s domesticity was a different breed. The corporate America of the supermarkets and giant food producers fed a conservative nostalgia for "Mom in the kitchen" in order to satisfy their need to build markets for more and more commercial products.

Cake mixes were introduced in 1949. Flour sifters were banished to the farthest corner of the cabinet, and "homemade" cakes came from a box. When market studies showed that women liked to feel as if they were actually doing some cooking, the manufacturers changed the process, allowing them the satisfaction of adding fresh eggs. But they went further. With embellishment, a cake mix could be the foundation of an elaborate concoction. The food manufacturers' consumer advisers came up with endless suggestions for ways to use their products so they would seem like our own.

In 1928 Missouri, Virginia Abney's Gold Cake got its richness from sixteen egg yolks, beaten in one at a time. Its 1950 counterpart was made from a simple yellow cake mix from Pillsbury combined with a package of lemon Jell-O, 3/4 cup of apricot nectar, 3/4 cup of salad oil, a tablespoon of lemon extract, and four eggs, separated (the whites beaten and folded in last). Baked for an hour and twenty minutes in an angel-cake pan, this turned into an impressive lemon cake (without any real lemons!). In the process, the time-saving attributes of the products were often lost. So, for many women, was the art of making a cake from scratch.

When we sang "If I'd Known You Were Coming I'd Have Baked a Cake," we might have been thinking of this. And when Bing Crosby crooned, "You ought to bake a Sunshine Cake / It really isn't so hard to make," we didn't rush to look up the six-egg recipe in *The Settlement Cook Book*; we opened a box.

Buffet suppers composed of made-ahead casseroles of "fork-only" food made it possible to expand social life past the limitations of tiny dining areas. "We didn't go out to eat so much," Joan McPherson remembers. "Maybe to an Italian or Chinese restaurant now and then." The parties at home followed a predictable pattern. Cocktails (real cocktails—no one drank wine) were accompanied by Clam Dunk or Lipton's Onion Soup Dip served with potato chips, cocktail franks wrapped in Pillsbury pie crust, or canned caponata. The main dish was an oversized casserole of Beef Stroganoff, Chicken Tetrazzini, or a favorite of mine called Witch House Stew (a dark, rich mixture of lentils and ground beef and tomatoes that cost very little to make and fed multitudes), accompanied by a salad and French bread with garlic or herb butter. The cookbooks were full of warnings—

"Men Like Meat" was still an article of faith. Men were also said to be suspicious of unfamiliar dishes that combined several ingredients, but perhaps these were served with such frequency that they ceased to be suspect.

For anxious hostesses, there were foolproof recipes. Mushrooms and Rice, a recipe from a cookbook called *Make It Now, Bake It Later*, calls for instant rice, salad oil, canned mushrooms, canned beef consomme, soy sauce, chopped green onions, salt and water. The trusty can opener that Poppy Cannon raised to cooking stardom is almost the only tool you need for this simple dish. Mixed in a casserole, the ingredients bake for half an hour or so. "Do not stir," the recipe instructs firmly.[10] Simple and clean as this recipe is, the book allows for the possibility of preparing it in advance (just don't add the liquid to the dry ingredients until it is time to bake).

Make It Now, Bake It Later and another favorite of mine, *Take It Easy before Dinner*, fit the picture of postwar domesticity. The object of a woman's effort was to please husband, children, and friends. It demanded skill in organization, in psychology, in nutrition, but the results were supposed to look effortless. The woman in the magazine kitchen was a cute, trim person, usually blonde, with a perfect unmussed page-boy hairdo and a little white apron tied around her tiny waist to protect her neatly pressed house dress from spills and splashes, or she might wear a cute cap-sleeved cotton print wraparound called a "Swirl." She almost never appears actually to be cooking; instead, she's triumphantly displaying a plate of cookies or a steaming casserole.

In cold war America, the effort of cooking was supposed to be concealed. The hot kitchen, the greasy or floury fingers, the sweaty brow were not meant to be seen. No one talked about "the servant problem" anymore and cookbooks no longer gave advice on how to entertain at luncheon without a maid, but there was still an unspoken idea that it was unseemly for ladies to be caught slaving in the kitchen. Women who eschewed the quick recipes and made complex casseroles that required a couple of hours' hard work nevertheless presented them as if they had appeared by magic. Cool and poised, the hostess brought forth from the oven a dish to set before her family and friends, modestly accepting compliments if compliments were offered, and breathing nothing of the work that had produced them.

Peeling real onions makes you cry. Real garlic smells up the house. So dried onions and garlic powder in little jars took their place. Real fresh mushrooms might come with dirt clinging to them or, worse, be past their prime and slimy, unlike the neat, dependable mushrooms available in little cans, already sliced or chopped. Hanging anxiously over a simmering pot of rice lest it burn could make one's face red. The truly perfect wife presented in the magazines knew how to cook wonderful meals (and keep the house clean, the laundry done, and the children happy) without any such *visible* effort.

Even if a woman chose to cook something messy, it was still possible to work the miracle. While her husband was at the office, while the children were at school or watching "Captain Kangaroo," while the baby napped, she performed the messy parts (if there were any)—browning meat, chopping carrots, peeling potatoes. Then the cook cleaned up the kitchen, washed her hands, combed her hair, put on lipstick, and at the right moment just slid that casserole into the oven.

I rarely risked such last-minute drama as a cheese soufflé, but I made good use of my old-fashioned iron pot. I made split-pea soup. My sister sent me a wonderful recipe for pot roast; the iron pot simmered it slowly in red wine and ginger (the ginger was optional, in case it seemed too exotic) until it was tender. I cooked Irish stew, Boeuf Bourguignon, goulash. All of these could be prepared ahead of time, though without using processed foods. But they offered me the occasional subversive pleasure of improvising. So real cooking survived, and when we women of the 1950s later woke up to the pleasures of making more complex dishes, we were not totally unprepared.

But for now, this was the heyday of the fantastic molded salads and desserts that the comedian Anna Russell brilliantly parodied in her monologue of a clubwoman proudly describing a meal that ended in her specialty, "my lime Jell-O, marshmallow, cottage cheese SURPRISE!" In Darien, a dessert recipe circulated, somewhat ominously called Broken Glass Jell-O—three colors of Jell-O cut in cubes and set in gelatin-stiffened whipped cream. Instant rice (first marketed in 1950) and mashed potatoes (1946) stood ready for use at a moment's notice. A twist of the wrist opened a cardboard cylinder and out popped biscuits, expanding as they burst from their container, ready to bake and serve. Gorton's frozen fish sticks appeared in 1955. Children loved them. The producers and advertisers of processed foods exploited the familiar while selling the time-saving aspects, freshness, and year-round availability of their products.

Menus had not changed all that much. Broiled or roasted chicken or an inexpensive loin of pork "on special" were mainstays of the week's dinners; the leftovers reappeared in casseroles with canned gravy. Frozen chicken pies opened to reveal chunks of chicken, peas, carrots, and potatoes swimming in pale yellow sauce, hardly a gourmet dish but cheap and easy to keep on hand. If no one was looking, even TV dinners, which came to the supermarkets in 1954, might serve, but the pretense was that these were for emergencies, such as when the woman of the house was sick or had to be away overnight.

Women did nearly all the cooking. A wife who was going away for a few days (even if her trip was to the hospital to have another baby) made sure the freezer was filled with enough meals to see her husband and children through. The exception to the gendered view of cooking and to the hidden preparation of food in advance was cooking outdoors. Men seldom approached the kitchen stove, but outdoor cooking on the charcoal braziers on legs that became standard equipment in suburban back yards—that was men's work. Here women deferred to their husbands, who liked to play with fire. The men were not inclined to consult a cookbook and in fact the cookbooks paid scant attention to this branch of meat preparation. The occasional cookbook devoted to grilled food, like *The Complete Book of Outdoor Cookery* by James Beard and Helen Evans Brown, published in 1955, was addressed to men: "We believe," wrote Beard and Brown, that charcoal cookery "is primarily a man's job and that a woman, if she's smart, will keep it that way."[11] For the most part, men learned by experience. Mastering the flames they had created with large douses of charcoal starter, they flipped hamburgers and hot dogs and the occasional steak or chicken. Unlike their wives, they performed publicly, demonstrating their skill to wide-eyed children and suitably impressed guests. Of course women provided the rest of the meal—macaroni salad (a package of instant macaroni made this simple), pickles, rolls, ketchup, mustard, potato chips, sliced tomatoes, and a baked dessert or brownies made from a mix.

Clever party desserts designed to fool the eye as well as please the palate were popular. One of these was something that, in Connecticut, was called Mock Apple Pie; some other names I've run across for it are Soda Cracker Pie, Georgia Cracker Pie (this in a Nashville cookbook), Mystery Torte (the recipe on the Nabisco Premium Saltine box), and in Iowa the cryptic E.E.E. Missouri pie. Fine cracker crumbs, nuts, sugar, egg whites, and a little cream of tartar or baking powder and vanilla flavoring are transformed in the oven into a delicate meringuelike concoction that vaguely tastes like apples; it takes well to a layer of whipped cream and possibly some fresh fruit. First-time tasters faced the challenge of guessing what the ingredients were, and they usually failed. This sounds like—and was—the perfect fifties dessert, but years after I first tasted it I found out that it had a history. It was invented by covered-wagon pioneers, a true example of making do with what is on hand—soda crackers.

Another transformation was an icebox cake made of Famous Chocolate Wafers (they were thin and crisp and in those days they came in a tall, chocolate-and-gold can, and nothing else would do) and whipped cream, layered together and chilled and then sliced on the diagonal. The zebra-striped slices had a French-bakery look and even tasted like a chocolate torte.

Our mothers had shopped at small local stores, but by now the A & P had built a supermarket close by; mine was in a shopping center on the Boston Post Road. By 1959 there were thirty-two thousand supermarkets in the United States; they accounted for 69 percent of all food-store sales. Most of them have been replaced; the occasional survivor looks as small by present-day superstore standards as the corner grocery looked in 1952 compared to them.

No grocer or butcher was on hand to advise, cajole, or bully as he had in the small groceries of the past. Pushing a shopping cart up and down the aisles, picking things off the shelf, comparing brand prices, watching our coupons, choosing our vegetables, all this we did alone. Marketing advice came silently but insistently from the displays and the packages and from supermarket magazines like *Woman's Day*, packed with menus and recipes that included the foods that would be the month's "best buys." The magazines urged menu planning and list making, and for the hopelessly disorganized, *Woman's Day* offered a monthly calendar of dinner menus.

Cookbooks, and especially magazines, encouraged planning menus before shopping, but in the store, artful displays and special offers urged impulse buying. The science of selling became more elaborate. Ever solicitous of the customer, supermarkets studied and catered to shoppers' desires and anxieties. At Grand Union headquarters, management decided, "Women are insecure about buying meat," and blamed this on "the time when the trade was cartooned in terms of the straw hat, the spotty apron, and the heavy thumb on the scale." To reassure shoppers, Grand Union put its clean, honest butchers, engaged in their sanitary work, on display; women selecting precut, prewrapped meat could look up and see, through a window behind the counter, the butcher trimming more pork chops.[12]

The prime target of the manufacturers and the supermarkets was the "Mrs. Consumer" of the fifties, the housewife with children who did not (in the phrase of the day) "go out to business," but made a career of homemaking. For her, Mary Ryan wrote, "the packaged foods of the '50s were advertised as methods of making cooking more elaborate and demanding, rather than simplifying the homemaker's job. Cake mixes were to be used 'creatively,' given a 'personal touch,' and required effort to expiate the 'underlying guilt' of the housewife who cut corners."[13] This extra complexity was supposed to make cooking a worthwhile endeavor for an educated woman.

Working women received little attention, although the number of working mothers increased 400 per cent between 1940 and 1960.[14] Most people, including their husbands, expected that these women would still produce dinner every night. For them, mixes and frozen foods played a different role, relieving a little of the pressure and allowing an alternative to the often-recommended system of spending the weekend cooking food for the coming week.

For the generation that formed all those young families in the fifties, the newly discovered unit with the timely name "nuclear family" was central. Men's careers supported it, women's home activities kept it healthy and intact, the suburban community confirmed it, and winning the cold war demanded it. In the kitchen and around the house women pleased themselves by imagining that they were self-sufficient, like settlers of new territories, doing everything for themselves. But it was as much pretense as the Mock Apple Pie. Technology was present everywhere. The construct was made possible by corporate manufacturers of frozen foods, tuna fish, kitchen appliances, pressure cookers, and blenders. The domestic life that 1950s America took such pride in was, to a large extent, packaged.

With the aid of technology, housewives had gained autonomy and did their own work without arduous labor. If the independence and self-sufficiency of families were illusory, their privacy and closeness were real. Women could and did pay close attention to raising their children; they valued caring and intimacy among husbands and wives and parents and children above almost everything. The food they prepared and set before their families might be ersatz home cooking but it was a genuine expression of such a priority. The cold-blooded good management techniques that had been applied to housekeeping in the 1920s and the warm concern for psychological welfare that characterized domestic advice of the 1930s came together in the 1950s.

The lives were as enclosed and complete unto themselves as the casseroles. Families lived among others like themselves, in an isolation almost as great as that generations ago on a Vermont or Missouri farm. Most of the baby sitters came from within the same development, and few wives could afford to hire someone to clean their houses. With rare exceptions white middle-class Americans living in the suburbs had little contact with recent immigrants or African Americans. Living in Old Greenwich, Connecticut, I knew that not far away in Stamford there were people who were poor, but I hardly ever saw them. Social problems had been left behind in the city, outside of my daily consciousness. The McCarthy hearings on television exposed me and my neighbors to cruelty in black and white, but at a distance. We would grow a few years older and more self-aware before we really felt the sharp pinch of responsibility for the social injustices we hadn't seen and barely knew about.

If people sheltered themselves from their poorer neighbors, they were kept aware of the enemy abroad. In the cold war, the ultimate in insularity and togetherness was the home bomb shelter. The Federal Civil Defense Administration, established in 1950, campaigned to persuade families to maintain their own shelters, stocked with nonperishable foods, in their basements, arguing that, thus prepared, they could survive an atomic bomb. A brochure giving detailed instructions and lists of supplies cast the shelter as an extension of old-fashioned domesticity. Once again a government agency grabbed for a metaphor. "Grandma's pantry was always ready," it said. "She was ready when the preacher came on Sunday or she was ready when the relatives arrived from Nebraska." The ghoulish parallel is obvious: you, too, could be prepared when a more ominous visitor, the Bomb, arrived.[15]

The self-sufficiency of the bomb shelter depended on the products of Campbell, Heinz, and Chicken-o'-the-Sea. Almost no one grew her own vegetables, let alone canned them, and chickens were not permitted in the suburbs. In Conneticut, I did not grow berries and make jam. Few of my neighbors baked bread at home. The clever combining of mass-produced ingredients was fun, but it didn't entirely satisfy the creative impulse.

The baby-boom babies started school. Their mothers began to suspect there was more to life than trying out the latest recipes on the Crisco can. The black humor of Roald Dahl's 1953 short story, "Lamb to the Slaughter," exposed the rage buried beneath the blandness of suburban life. Mary Maloney, the central character, is a stay-at-home wife pregnant with her first child. When her husband comes home and tells her he's leaving the marriage, she, stunned and enraged, hits him over the head with a frozen leg of lamb that had been intended for his dinner. When the police come to investigate his death, the lamb is roasting in the oven; the perfect hostess, she persuades them to eat the murder weapon.[16] Patrick Maloney had violated the unwritten contract of the marriage; his wife's passive service to her husband suddenly turned to violent wrath.

In the 1954 *Brown v. Board of Education* decision the Supreme Court redefined equality, and pointed the way to the civil rights movement of the 1960s. That call for equality led to another awakening, the women's movement of our times. In 1963, Betty Friedan revealed the results of her survey of her Smith College classmates and others in *The Feminine Mystique*. The packaged life, it appeared, was less than perfect.

Both American cooking and the culture of suburbia had become safe, but they were dangerously boring. There was little art and less science to opening cans of condensed soup and breaking eggs into batches of cake mix. Women began to recognize the negative aspects of imprisonment in even a high-tech kitchen. Their restlessness found a spokesperson in Betty Friedan. But home cooking may have been rescued by a new champion: Julia Child.

CHAPTER SEVEN

Boeuf Bourguignon and Chocolate Mousse

O N F E B R U A R Y 1 1, 1 9 6 3, A T A L L, S L I G H T L Y S T O O P E D W O M A N W I T H A S T E A D Y G A Z E A N D A C O N F I D E N T A I R L O O K E D O U T from the black and white television screen and began to explain, in a high-pitched, breathless voice that would soon become instantly recognizable, how to cook Boeuf Bourguignon. "The French Chef" had arrived in the kitchen. Julia Child was here, and cooking hasn't been the same since. But behind her triumph lies a good deal of history.

At the turn of the twentieth century, American cookbooks and cooking schools taught American cooking—a style that drew heavily on plain New England cooking, with a dose of German. Immigrant women who hoped for jobs in American kitchens learned along with women who were native born. Similarly, well-meaning social workers tried to persuade recent arrivals to cook and eat American food. Immigrant children, the reasoning went, attended school where they learned to speak English and to be Americans. Taking that message of both language and mores to their homes and families was more difficult than preaching it in the classroom. Adult immigrants could not be sent to school; they might at least be assimilated at the table.

Strangers in a strange land, first-generation immigrants did not willingly change their eating habits. They saw no reason to give up the comfort of familiar food from their country of origin. But the voice of authority, intent on propagating a single American culture, disapproved. "Still eating spaghetti, not yet assimilated," a social worker reported after a visit with an Italian family in the early years of the century.[1]

Grocery stores in Italian neighborhoods in Boston, New York, and Philadelphia, sold olive oil, pasta, and braided strings of garlic. Local bakers filled their windows in the morning with fresh round or oval loaves of bread. The more adventurous city dwellers might visit these neighbors now and then, enjoying the exotic sights and smells, and take home a loaf of bread or a wedge of cheese. They visited similar ethnic neighborhoods—Hungarian, Portuguese, Chinese, and others—in other parts of the city. Meanwhile, people whose families had established an earlier foothold and a more substantial income were hiring new immigrants as cooks and teaching them to prepare Yankee pot roast or fried chicken. In dual-language cookbooks (aimed at servants to the middle class) American recipes appeared in English and Chinese, or other languages, providing Americanization and language instruction simultaneously. The emphasis was on a white Protestant American norm.

When I was a child, my German American grandmother still cooked plump and filling dumplings with her chicken stew, following a custom that came with her family to America. But my other grandmother, separated from her Scottish and Irish ancestors by generations of New Yorkers, depended on an Irish cook to bring forth from the kitchen what the family enjoyed eating—the all-American roast beef and mashed potatoes, and, on occasion, in emulation of the fine New York restaurants, asparagus elegantly dressed with hollandaise sauce.

In contrast to the "all-American" cookbooks, Lizzie Black Kander's unabashedly Jewish *Settlement Cook Book*, first published in Milwaukee in 1901, met its readers halfway. Kander was one of a group of Jewish women who organized Milwaukee's first social settlement. There, in the midst of night school classes, music groups, mothers' clubs and gymnasium activities, she taught young women to cook. It became convenient to print the recipes instead of having her students copy them by hand, and so her cookbook was born. From an initial printing of one thousand copies, the book grew and expanded; it became the source of funds for the settlement, and eventually, in 1931, financed the building of a new Jewish community center. Many editions later, it still bears its subtitle, "The Way to a Man's Heart."

Although Kander taught American housekeeping methods and ideas about nutrition, she did not insist that her students cast aside Jewish food traditions. Lamb stew and New England boiled dinner share space with Gaenseklein (fricasseed goose), and the dessert section is rich with noodle puddings and matzos charlottes. A chapter entitled "Kuchen (Coffee Cakes)" includes Kipfel, Purim Cakes, Kolatchen, and Schnecken. All this as well as an array of Passover dishes made the book a classic among Milwaukee's Jewish population and Jewish families around the country.

More often, xenophobia prevailed. In 1938, Katherine Kellock, the editor of the Federal Writers' Project book, *U.S. One: Maine to Florida*, worried that American regional cooking was disappearing. She urged travelers to ask for local specialties in restaurants in order to encourage their survival. Kellock minced no words in condemning American attempts at foreign cooking. "Few American cooks are entirely successful in following French recipes and few French cooks can cook a typical American meal," she wrote. "A blighting influence on American cooking has been the attempt to impose French menus on the American people without an understanding of French methods and the use of French ingredients."[2]

American cookbooks, not outspokenly patriotic, were cautious about ethnic recipes; when they appeared at all, it was in a far-from-literal translation of the original. When *Time* magazine published a cookbook based on readers' submissions in 1949, a small selection of "international recipes" appeared at the end. The editors reassured their audience that while these dishes were "exotic enough to intrigue your guests," they were "not *too* exotic to alarm their palates."[3] The ingredients of *Make It Now, Bake It Later*'s 1961 "Chinese" casserole included canned tuna and mushroom soup (again!), soy sauce, cashew nuts, canned mushrooms and canned Chinese chow mein noodles, minced onion and chopped celery, all mixed together in a casserole and baked.[4] In other words, it was a rough translation of tuna-noodle casserole. A Chinese visitor would have been baffled, if not alarmed. Genuine Chinese cooking requires much chopping and slicing of ingredients and quick cooking in hot oiled pans just before serving, techniques not in fashion at that time in American kitchens.

Italian pasta (in its infinite variety) and freshly grated Parmesan cheese had been diminished, in American kitchens, into macaroni and cheese. This American classic was a long way from its Italian origins; when it didn't come fully prepared from a can or box, it could be— and usually was—made with processed cheese and condensed soup. Spaghetti sauces (for those who went beyond opening a can of Chef Boy-ar-dee spaghetti with red sauce) were mostly debased versions of the rich Bolognese, made with hamburger and canned tomatoes, or canned tomato sauce, or tomato soup, or even ketchup. Both Italian and Chinese cooking at home were compromised by American unfamiliarity with cooking in oil.

The willingness to compromise stemmed from ignorance of the real thing. Standard cookbooks, magazines, and advertisements for canned ingredients all encouraged the acceptance of approximations. Much later, in the 1980s, I—and thousands of other American cooks— would discover Marcella Hazan and the pleasures of rigatoni baked with a meat sauce that had simmered for four hours, mingled with béchamel and sprinkled with a few tablespoons of roughly grated Reggiano Parmesan and a little butter. In the fifties, "Italian," when it didn't mean spaghetti with ground beef and tomato sauce, might be Fannie Farmer's Jo Mazzotti, a casserole that included ground pork, canned tomato soup, mushrooms, celery, green peppers, lemon juice, and a large amount of sharp Cheddar cheese, layered with noodles and baked. The recipe only hinted of Italy; condensed soup and factory-made tomato sauce substituted for simple ingredients and hours of cooking. I often made Jo Mazzotti; from my point of view it satisfied the important criteria for party food—it was prepared ahead of time, was a robust main dish that, accompanied by bread and salad, fed ten or twelve people, and guests could easily eat it with a fork while sitting on the couch or on the floor, or even while standing up. For the time being, although I didn't know who Jo Mazzotti might have been, he or she was a household hero.

I may have come closer to authenticity with the French cheese fondue we made in the chafing dish we, like almost every young couple in the fifties, received as a wedding present. (As far as I know, these chafing dishes were never used for anything else.) Our recipe had come to us by a circuitous route from Charlotte Turgeon, a well-known teacher of French cooking who happened to live in a college town, via a fraternity where it was a feature of the annual and rowdy "French Night." In the far more sedate atmosphere of newlywed entertaining we proudly prepared it at the table, over a can of Sterno—one of the very few moments when we allowed the act of cooking to be visible. Unlike the sober casseroles, fondue, eaten with hunks of bread speared on skewers and dunked into the melted cheese, is also a food that invites a certain amount of playfulness.

This bit of Gallic exoticism may have been a forerunner of interest in true ethnic cooking, but in general, blandness reigned. Foods with a "foreign flavor" lacked any authenticity. The turn-of-the-century social worker who had urged immigrants to eat American had carried the day; meat and potatoes were king.

––––––––––

A generation of American children had grown up eating vegetables that came from the freezer in little rectangular boxes—their mothers, who had known the tedium of paring potatoes, French-cutting green beans, and shelling peas, were delighted with rigid blocks of mashed potatoes and beans all ready for boiling water. By the time these children became parents, they took such things as a matter of course. Between 1950 and 1970 the number of items handled by a typical supermarket rose from 3,750 to 7,800. New varieties of canned soup, frozen dinners and cakes, and packaged mixes accounted for many of those items. But other areas of the store languished.

Frozen vegetables allowed greater choice, especially in winter, but in the fresh produce section, limited variety discouraged exploration of other cuisines. When the choice was limited to iceberg or romaine lettuce in the market, it was not possible to do anything very exciting in the way of salad. Caesar salad—romaine lettuce with garlic-flavored croutons and pregrated Parmesan, dressed with oil and lemon juice and a raw egg—came east from California as a popular "sophisticated" alternative to the ever-present wedge of iceberg draped in Russian dressing. No kiwi fruit or bean sprouts or daikon radishes or radicchio or bok choy brightened the produce displays. A shopper could not count on finding fresh mushrooms in good condition any time she wanted them; she might find only a miserable heap of dark, exhausted, withered fungi lurking in a basket.

Specials on pork or chicken were miraculously coupled with compilations of recipes in women's magazines (especially the supermarket publications) offering dozens of ways to cook them. A typical issue of *Woman's Day,* in January 1960, presented a collection of fifty recipes for pork. The basic roast pork and broiled chops led off. The other recipes depended heavily on canned and bottled ingredients for their exotic effect: Pork Hawaiian (canned pineapple tidbits, vinegar, soy sauce, sugar, and green pepper); Pork Oriental (canned mushrooms, celery, green onions, canned mixed Chinese vegetables, and corn starch—accompanied by rice or chow mein noodles); Georgia Pork Chops (peanut butter and mushroom soup); Herb-stuffed Chops (poultry seasoning); and Spicy Pork (frozen orange juice, brown sugar, cinnamon, salt, and paprika).[5]

By 1966, when the magazine did a reprise of the pork theme, times had changed. The recipes, considerably more sophisticated, appeared under an international label: "A Treasury of Recipes from Many Lands." History set the atmosphere: "In most parts of the world cooks have been concocting savory pork recipes for hundreds of years. In this impressive collection you will see how each nation brings its own special tastes to the preparation of pork. From Mexico and the Mediterranean countries come highly seasoned dishes; the Hungarians give us their love of paprika and dumplings; the Indians flavor pork with curry, the Japanese with soy sauce, the Chinese with sweet-and-sour sauce."[6] And so on—Italian, Hungarian, Australian, Irish, Polish, culminating in Chinese Pork and Smoked Oysters.

In the summer of that year, *Woman's Day* exoticized the most American of meats, the hot dog, in an issue that featured Frankfurter-Apricot Curry with Rice.[7] I spare you the recipe, but as I already confessed I had a fistful of exotic frankfurter recipes in my file, clipped from *Woman's Day* and other magazines in the hope of expanding my children's taste horizons by starting with something they liked.

Before World War II, few Americans had traveled widely enough to know the difference between ersatz ethnic food and the real thing. Sophisticated city people had a taste for fashionable dishes like Beef Stroganoff, sukiyaki, and French omelettes. But the war took many Americans to Europe. In the course of their military service they learned to appreciate a new range of tastes. In the postwar period, business lunches in expense-account restaurants familiarized men with European cooking. More people traveled abroad. Slowly "foreign" food came to seem less strange. By the time Marion Rombauer Becker began working on the major revision that eventually became the 1963 edition of *The Joy of Cooking*, she understood, as Anne Mendelson has written, "that an all-purpose manual for American housewives not only could but should count on their being interested in cassoulet, couscous, stuffed grape leaves, salade niçoise, navarin printanier, enchiladas, fish quenelles, and turkey mole."[8]

The American Dream is not about standing still. It's about exploring—lighting out for the Territory. The process of widening horizons had begun. Coca Cola cake was a great novelty, but the novelty wore off. In the sixties, suburban women with two or three or four children in school—and perhaps at least a part-time job as well—found adventure where they could, often in the kitchen. My friend June Ball recalls joining a cookbook-of-the-month club. "We had a month of San Francisco cooking, following a month of every conceivable kind of bread, followed by *Lessons in Gourmet Cooking*, followed by *Casserole Treasury*, followed by *The Book of Meat*, followed by *The Gold Cook Book*" (by the well-known French chef improbably named Louis de Gouy). Her mail brought collections of Irish, Israeli, Chinese, Spanish, Jewish, English, and Hungarian recipes—the last, by the inimitable Jolie Gabor, requiring robust quantities of cream, sour cream, butter, and eggs. "This went on for a couple of years," she remembers, and her husband "occasionally would wish for the same thing twice." In the kitchen cabinets fondue pots, chafing dishes, salad molds, and bundt pans accumulated.[9]

I, too, belonged to a cookbook club. When I went to the city I often made an expedition to New York's Second Avenue, where Papri-kas Weiss, the only source I knew in those days for real Hungarian rose paprika, was located, and I brought home a precious cardboard container of it to use for months in goulash and veal paprika. While much of the ethnic cooking I did in those days was adapted to Ameri-can ingredients, this was one dish that could plausibly be called au-thentic.

As this wave of ethnic recipes swept in during the early sixties, few dishes achieved such authenticity. Many were timid adaptations designed not to shock the bland taste buds of American diners. Famil-iar, readily available ingredients were often substituted for the real thing, and canned ingredients stood in for fresh. *The Complete Electric Skillet–Frypan Cookbook*, one of many that promoted a particular appli-ance as the all-purpose answer to cooking needs, had recipes for suki-yaki and Coq au Vin, made at the table in no time. It also gave directions for something called Easy Cheese Blintzes, made with thin-sliced white bread, and suggested completing the meal by heating cof-fee and flaming brandy in the skillet to produce Café Brulot.[10] Only the names remained to hint of Old Russia or a Parisian salon.

Some cooks wanted the real thing. For them, Doubleday and Company published a series of ethnic cookbooks. They invited read-ers to learn "The Art of . . . [French, Greek, Sicilian, Italian, or other] Cooking." These volumes, typical of their period, were small in size and usually opened with an evocation of the culture and food, the feasts, the grandmothers, the kitchen smells. The recipes were concise and authentic, measurements were exact, and glossaries, wine sugges-tions, and lists of suppliers of ingredients were often included. The books were written by cooks or food writers, usually Americans de-scended from the group they were writing about. (An interesting ex-ception was *The Art of Greek Cookery*, a church cookbook privately published by the women of St. Paul's Greek Orthodox Church in Hempstead, Long Island, which caught the attention of the food edi-tors at the *New York Times*. When the *Times* published some recipes from the collection it created a large demand for the book. Doubleday picked it up and published an expanded version.) The series, as its titles indicate, promoted the art, not the science, of cooking. No nutritional information appeared in its pages, but most of them included a list of appropriate wines.

In the cosy French restaurants of American cities, Boeuf Bourguignon was a standby, along with Soupe à l'Oignon and red checked tablecloths. Its migration into American kitchens offers a remarkable illustration of the confusion of approaches to international cooking.

In 1941, in the first issue of the new *Gourmet* magazine, a quiz for restaurant-savvy readers, "Do You Know Your Menu and Cookery Terms?" asked them to identify Boeuf Bourguignon, along with Coq au Chambertin, Poulet en Cocotte, and seven ways of preparing pheasant. A year later, in the winter of 1942, *Gourmet* brought Boeuf Bourguignon to American home kitchens as a refugee from the war in Europe. Samuel Chamberlain, writing under the pen name Phineas Beck, described the hilly wine country of Nuits-St. Georges and the aroma of "something exotic and supremely flavorful" simmering on the back of the stove in a French kitchen. Then, having evoked the atmosphere, he introduced his French cook, Clémentine (he never mentioned her surname), who had taken refuge from the war with her American employers.

He shared with his readers Clémentine's recipe for Boeuf Bourguignon.

In an iron casserole bubbling with 2 tablespoons butter, brown 2 pounds good lean stewing beef, cut into 1 1/2-inch cubes, until the meat is 'closed.' Remove the meat, add 1 tablespoon flour, and make a *roux brun*. Add salt and pepper, and 1 1/2 cups good dry red wine. Slice 1/2 pound small onions, a carrot, 1/2 cup mushrooms, a clove of garlic, and 6 shallots. Brown 2/3 of the onions separately in butter. Return the meat to the casserole, and add the sliced vegetables and a *bouquet garni* composed of parsley, thyme, and bay leaf. Add a veal knuckle, if one is obtainable. Add also 1/2 cup Madeira if you have some, and enough water to bring the liquid level with the meat.

Put the lid on this poetic ensemble and allow it to simmer very gently from 3 to 4 hours, until the meat is tender. Half an hour before serving add a liqueur glass of brandy. Strain the vegetables from the dark russet-red sauce before serving.[11]

Gourmet readers presumably were familiar with terms like *roux brun* and *bouquet garni* and the recipe, accompanied by boiled rice and the recommended "vigorous red wine," was sure to please their bistro-loving palates.

But this stew, now basic to our cooking repertoire, remained for the most part the province of chefs and elitist publications for another decade. Then, as it crept into the pages of women's magazines and cookbooks, the classic dish underwent strange transformations. When "Beef Bourguignon" finally made its appearance in the ninth edition of Fannie Farmer's all-American *Boston Cooking-School Cook Book* in 1951, potatoes and mushrooms were unceremoniously dumped in the pot for the last forty-five minutes of five hours, not simmering fragrantly on the back of the stove, but cooking in a slow (250°) oven. This looks more like the familiar Irish stew with a little (one cup) of wine thrown in—certainly nothing that would alarm an American family. American cookbooks generally did not mention either cognac or Madeira. Even the wine was sometimes "optional" or included apologetically, along with the assurance that the alcohol evaporates in the cooking.

A letter to *Gourmet* published in April 1954 shows the slow progress of change. Dorothy M. Birk of Cleveland wrote to the editors of *Gourmet*, "I have been trying to find the recipe for beef with Burgundy for some time and would appreciate it greatly if you could help." *Gourmet*, graciously not pointing out that she had missed the earlier recipe, responded with a recipe similar to Clémentine's, but ample enough to feed twelve.[12] By the time the news reached Cleveland, the Burgundian marvel had become standard fare at dinner parties and buffet suppers on the East Coast. Clémentines graced few kitchens, but people who did their own party cooking appreciated the advantages of a dish that could be prepared in advance, that would even gain flavor over a day or two, and that was easy to warm up and required only simple accompaniments—a salad, French bread (seldom called baguettes in those days), and, perhaps, some rice, noodles, or potatoes. This was followed by what one friend of ours, an amiable and frequent guest at neighborhood dinners, ruefully called "the inevitable Chocolate Mousse."

As Boeuf Bourguignon became de rigeur at suburban dinner parties, authenticity took a back seat to convenience. Not every cook cared whether the recipe was classic; they looked for simplified methods of getting a company dinner on the table. Community cookbooks, which often reveal underground cooking secrets, suggested shortcuts. *An Uncommon Cook Book* published in Stamford, Connecticut, in 1978 to benefit the Easter Seal Rehabilitation Center, began its "Beef Burgundy" by marinating the meat in wine overnight before browning and cooking it in standard fashion, and ended by topping the stew with *canned* potatoes, onions, and carrots and baking for half an hour. Worse was in store. Another recipe turned up in community cookbooks of the seventies and eighties, a heresy with only five ingredients: beef, a can of cream of mushroom soup, a miserly half cup of red wine, an envelope of Lipton Onion Soup Mix, and a four-ounce can of mushrooms! "Mix soup, onion soup mix, mushrooms and wine and stir well," advised one good neighbor in Dover, New Hampshire. "Add to meat and coat all pieces well. Put in a covered casserole and bake in 300 degree oven for 3 hours. A little longer if you desire. DO NOT PEEK!" Presumably it's best not to look until this gummy-sounding mixture has coagulated beyond recognition.[13]

The struggle between authenticity and convenience goes on, and in the anxious and overcommitted nineties another element entered in as fat became an issue. Barbara Kafka introduced her "skinny" microwave Boeuf Bourguignon in 1989—no butter, just two teaspoons of vegetable oil, 256 calories, and 77 milligrams of cholesterol. But this gets us ahead of our story. In the sixties, it was Julia Child who took command of Boeuf Bourguignon.

In 1961, Jacqueline and John F. Kennedy came to the White House. The Kennedys hired a French chef, René Verdon; the appointment drew Craig Claiborne's approbation in the *New York Times*. In emulation of the Kennedy life style, French cooking came to be accepted as fun and only a delicious bit pretentious. By 1963 *Woman's Day* was publishing a collection called "Stews and Ragouts"— ragouts!—including an admittedly complicated French recipe, Daube de Boeuf, which required using a larding needle to insert a lardoon (a strip of salt pork rolled in a mixture of garlic, parsley, thyme, and cognac) in each cube of beef. The meat was marinated in wine with co-gnac and a bouquet of herbs before cooking.[14]

To many Americans "French" implies elegance and sophistica-tion at least as much as nationality. When French immigrants came to the United States, they came, not in masses like the Irish and the Italians, but as individuals. Many French immigrants found work in urban restaurants. French women were in demand as sales people in upmarket shops to provide an atmosphere of refinement and good taste.

Americans who wanted to eat French food found it in restau-rants (usually in large cities) and at exceptionally elaborate dinner par-ties. French cookbooks existed in English and Dione Lucas offered courses to ambitious New York gourmets and demonstrations on tele-vision. The Kennedys made French food seem glamorous. But Julia Child was determined, as she later told a reporter for *Time* magazine, "to take French cooking out of cuckoo land and bring it down to where everybody is."[15] No one knew that this one small step would lead to a national change in people's perceptions of cooking.

An exuberant, tall, and lanky Californian, a graduate of Smith College, Julia McWilliams was working in Washington when she met Paul Child. They were married in 1946 and began their life together there. According to her biographer, she was "not a natural or instinc-tive cook." She taught herself cooking, primarily from *The Joy of Cook-ing*, and she subscribed to *Gourmet*. She experimented, not always with great results; her college roommate recalled visiting for a meal that included an inedible kidney pie.[16]

Since Paul Child's government job took them abroad, Julia Child did not experience 1950s American cooking. During their years in Paris, she focused her enormous natural enthusiasm on learning classic French cooking. She took courses at the Cordon Bleu cooking school and practiced fervently. Two French friends, Simone Beck and Louisette Bertholle, were compiling a cookbook for Americans. Their publisher insisted that they have an American collaborator, and Child began testing recipes. "It was her job to rewrite the original technical instructions and get everything into readable English." Child's task was to work out American measurements, make sure ingredients were available in the United States, and write foolproof directions. But with her participation, the book soon changed from a collection of French recipes to "a book for American home cooks that would present cuisine bourgeoise using the techniques of haute cuisine, the techniques she had learned at Cordon Bleu."[17] She tested recipes in whatever category she was working on—chicken, for example, night after night, cooked in many ways and served to her husband and friends—in order to select the appropriate few. The book, *Mastering the Art of French Cooking*, became the printed equivalent of a cooking course. Like Irma Rombauer, whose style she greatly admired, Child was dissatisfied with the traditional format of recipes; on the book's generous pages ingredients and utensils were listed in bold type in the wide margin, grouped as they were to be used; the directions were on the right. If necessary, recipes ran for several pages. A good teacher, Child frequently built on a "master recipe," beginning by teaching how to do a roast chicken, for instance, and following the basic recipe with several variations.

Someone at WGBH, Boston's public television station, had watched Julia Child make an omelette on a book-review show and saw possibilities. Asked if she would be interested in doing a show on public television, Child responded, "I think we could make an interesting, adult series of half-hour TV programs of French cooking addressed to an intelligent, reasonably sophisticated audience which likes good food and cooking." And why should it be French? "Because," Julia Child said, "the French have treated cooking as a serious profession as well as an art, they are far more precise about their methods than any other national group. But as these methods are basic to all types of cooking, one will be a better cook in Spanish, Russian, or Italian if one has had French training."[18]

The first program, filmed in January and shown in February 1963, featured none other than Boeuf Bourguignon, along with Onion Soup, Lobster à l'Américaine, and Crêpes Suzette—dishes that any American who had ever eaten in a French restaurant would recognize. Child's approach to Boeuf Bourguignon was uncompromising; Clémentine would surely have approved.

In the series, as in *Mastering the Art of French Cooking*, Child emphasized techniques that were applicable to other dishes. By 1960, fifty million households had television. On television, she could *show* her audience how to do it—a return to the way people had learned to cook for generations, by watching their mothers, grandmothers, aunts, or the woman next door in action. The medium overcame the limitations imposed by the printed page; the clumsiness of explaining in words how physical tasks were done and how to judge the product was overcome.

She convinced her audience that you didn't have to be rich or sophisticated or a city dweller to poach a chicken properly and that such a basic task could be very satisfying. Inspired by watching "The French Chef," a more ambitious follower might stuff the bird with a rice, mushroom, and chicken liver mixture called Farce Évocation d'Albuféra, serve it with Sauce Supreme au Cari (curry sauce)—and enjoy a triumph.[19]

The audience, however, was different from Betty Crocker's or Fannie Farmer's. Child never made the housewife the focus of her attention, and if there was any message involving duty, it was simply, "Do it the right way." Indeed, to viewers who complained that she didn't do enough "plain cooking" she replied, "our program is for people who really like to cook . . . plain old housewives get plenty of encouragement and recipes from the daily newspapers."[20]

Statements such as this were perceived by some as an insult to housewives. In an attempt at diplomacy Child answered one such criticism, from a woman in Scarsdale, "Perhaps both terms, cooking and housewife, should be given new names, since the art of raising a family and maintaining a home with an ideal environment is of the highest order"—like the art of cooking.[21]

Julia Child addressed any individual who wanted to cook good food—whether or not they had ever wielded a spatula. Her personality, her humor, and her philosophy of cooking overcame distance. For her followers, she became not only a hero, but a friend as well. And many of the followers were indeed housewives. "From the beginning I liked you," wrote Veronica Foley of the Bronx, but at first I did not think I wanted to learn "French" cooking as I thought it was "fancy." . . . However I grew more and more enchanted with your ideas and I have learned many things of a practical nature that I can apply to simple everyday tasks—even such things as how to wash and store lettuce and other greens. . . . You can't imagine how much it helps everything to be able to watch how someone else copes with problems in the kitchen. . . . I want to thank you for being you and being so generous with your instructions, and for bringing joy to what had been lonely, baffling work, and for being my friend.[22]

Others were men, surprised to find themselves in the kitchen. Jim Kitchak of Racine, Wisconsin, wrote, "You have shown me that even I, a thirty-five year old, married man with two children, can design, prepare and present great food, and *enjoy* doing it!" Susan Marcum wrote, " my husband never took great interest in the culinary arts until he began watching your program. . . . I am deep in your debt, for my husband has grown and expanded into an area that has helped him become more of a well-rounded human being. He can take *any* recipe and improvise and not make it come out less than great."[23]

Young cooks took courage from her program. A boy of fifteen confessed that cooking was his "foremost hobby, past-time, and pleasure . . . (don't tell my friends that). . . . I'll make your Charlotte Malakoff tomorrow afternoon after school for Thanksgiving." A girl named Susan Rumsfield wrote to ask for "Something a nine year old could make by herself," and received recipes for a spaghetti dinner, Apples Alaska, and Strawberry Soufflé.[24]

Julia Child encouraged her audience, not only because she seemed to be enjoying herself but also because she was human enough to make a mistake. Unlike the authors of the classic cookbooks, concealed behind the printed page, seldom revealing a hint of personality (except for Irma Rombauer, from whose anecdotes there certainly emerged a person with a sense of humor), omniscient and unlikely ever to have made a mistake (again Rombauer is the exception, admitting to having "sacrificed many a burnt offering"), Child made mistakes, dropped things, and joked about it. "Never apologize," was her

motto. Those who watched her demonstrating how to make quenelles, those delicate cylinders of puréed fish mixed with cream and
truffles and poached in stock, will not forget how she told her viewers
not to panic if the mixture turned out too soft to poach. Just put it in
a ring mold, she advised, and call it fish soufflé!

This was all great fun and it produced great food, but what message was it sending to women who were beginning to be uncomfort-
able in their homemaker roles? Betty Friedan issued her clarion call,
The Feminine Mystique, in 1963, the same year that Julia Child started
her television career. The women who had been doing the household
work in private and presenting the results as a fait accompli were wak-
ing up. They had other things besides food on their minds. When
Steven Mintz and Susan Kellogg studied changes in American families they found that "in 1950, 25 percent of married women living
with their husbands worked outside the home; in the late 1980s the
figure is nearly 60 percent."[25] Many of the women who had gone
straight from school to marriage and childbearing were ready for public lives when all their children were in school. They were rightly tired
of being told that they must stay at home and be good consumers.
They felt confined, locked in to the duty of cooking and to traditional
ways of doing it. Cookbooks and home economists as well as corporate food producers had taken away much of the individual initiative
that had made Mrs. Abney and her friends proud. Instead, for many
women, the kitchen stove was a symbol of their imprisonment.

While Friedan was telling the world about "the problem that
had no name," reporting the claustrophobia of women who believed
that they were supposed to be satisfied with washing the kitchen floor,
changing diapers, and making meat loaf, Child was inviting women and
men to share her delight in the fine cooking that might or might not
require considerable time and attention, not as a duty but as a thoughtful pursuit. At first glance, these two messages that shared a moment
in time appear to be in conflict. But Friedan and Child, in different ways, both argued for empowerment of the individual. Both re-
futed the idea that gender must govern occupation. Unlike earlier
cookbook authors—Fannie Farmer, Lizzie Kander, and Irma Rombauer—Julia Child was not concerned with helping housewives get

through the daily effort of putting meals on the table, let alone with urging them to meet specific nutritional standards. There was no mention of serving and pleasing husbands. Men were welcome in the kitchen. She was engaged in teaching an honorable (and potentially great) craft and techniques that, once mastered, could be used creatively.

Women no longer believed they should conceal their effort, pretending there was a servant in the kitchen. If they chose to cook, they wanted credit for it. Some people who had considered cooking only drudgery even began to see its possibilities as a performance art. Kitchens grew larger or were attached to family rooms, reducing the isolation of the cook. The pleasure of cooking became a dominant theme. One admirer wrote to Julia Child, "The other night I had trouble sleeping—so at 3:30 A.M. I turned to page 454 [of *From Julia Child's Kitchen*] and started a batch of bread. As usual, whenever I use your marvelous recipes, it turned out fragrant and fabulous."[26]

The fashion in cooking set off by Julia Child may be said to have raised the bar for many people who might have been perfectly happy with conventional American cooking, bringing out the competitor or the overachiever or the perfectionist and leading inevitably to more time and work in the kitchen. Many feminists believed they had greater things to do than bake bread. But along with Craig Claiborne, Pierre Franey, and others, Child made sophisticated cooking seem accessible and she encouraged not only the appreciation but also the practice of cooking the food of other cultures.

Other changes had a part in this. Even the transience of Americans in midcentury may have made "foreign" food seem less foreign. Americans were traveling abroad more, and food was part of the adventure. Immigration laws that since the 1920s had kept strict control over the number and nationality of new arrivals were relaxed (for a while) by the Immigration and Naturalization Act of 1965, which abolished the system of national-origins quotas and established skills and reuniting of families as criteria for entry. New arrivals brought new foods. Those who couldn't travel found that exploring the food of other countries was a pleasing and accessible alternative way of experiencing other cultures. Craig Claiborne's *New York Times Cookbook*

(1961) opened with three paté recipes from Paris bistros and went on to an international array that included Indian chick peas, Cacciucco (the delicious Italian seafood stew), Pots de Crème au Chocolat, and Linzer Torte.

As corporations transferred their employees from one part of the country to another, foreignness became relative. "I am a Displaced Damn Yankee from Illinois," wrote one woman to Julia Child, "and have been tremendously home sick, here in the Deep South. They consider themselves the best cooks in the world, and look down their noses when I say I am not overly fond of Black eyed peas, grits, hog jowl, turnip greens, and congealed salad. That word congealed makes me think of blood, but that is what they call any salad that has gelatine in it."[27] For this woman, at least, French cooking, presented in Child's terms as a sort of universal fine cooking, offered an escape from the alien food around her. I wonder what her new neighbors thought of her Poularde Pochée à l'Estragon, her Courgettes Farcies aux Amandes, or her Tarte aux Pommes.

The approximations of the first wave of ethnic cookbooks yielded to a demand for authenticity. Often authentic recipes were difficult to achieve; the written recipe with exact measurements is, after all, largely a product of American obsession with science. In Italy, in China, in India, the transmission of cooking tradition takes place in families and regions from generation to generation without written records. Translating this into recognizable American cooking terms was a major task.

Grace Zia Chu, educated at Ginling College, Nanking, and Wellesley, had lived in the United States since 1941, and taught classes in Chinese cooking at the China Institute in America, the Mandarin House School of Cookery, Riverside Church, and in her own New York City apartment. According to Craig Claiborne she had "taught hundreds of New York men and women the joys of Chinese cuisine" before her 1962 book, *The Pleasures of Chinese Cooking*, was published. "There is probably no one on the New York scene who has done more to familiarize the public with the food of her homeland than Madame Grace Chu," wrote Claiborne.[28] Like Child, she had developed recipes that used ingredients available in American supermarkets, but she grouped them in one section of the book while another section's recipes required shopping at Chinese food stores. This book was a far cry from earlier collections like *The House of Chan Cookbook*, where the recipes had been so adapted to American supermarket tastes and ingredients as to bear little resemblance to real Chinese food. As many serious introductions to Chinese cooking have done since, Chu's book included careful, illustrated instructions on the use of a Chinese cleaver to cut up vegetables properly.

Joyce Chen, who opened her restaurant in Cambridge in 1958, published *The Joyce Chen Cook Book* in the same year. Like Grace Chu, she carefully explained the ingredients and techniques of Chinese cooking, but she adapted to American ingredients only when absolutely necessary.

People who lived in cities with Chinese, Italian, or Indian neighborhoods had access to the necessary array of spices and other ingredients, but the supermarkets lagged behind the trend in cooking. In 1961, when Julia Child and her two French coauthors published *Mastering the Art of French Cooking*, they acknowledged that in the United States canned mushrooms were sometimes the only ones available. They recommended enhancing their flavor by tossing them in a skillet with shallots and butter. Fresh leeks, another staple of French cooking, were seldom to be found. When food writers mentioned them at all, they advised cooks to snap them up when they saw them, sauté them in butter, and freeze them against the day that they might want to make vichyssoise (an American invention, it must be said) for a dinner party.

Gradually, the interest of cooks in ethnic cooking began to influence the stock of supermarkets. Business recognized the arrival of the gourmet consumer. Supermarket produce sections changed, responding to demand. In 1967, Mrs. Merle Smith Jr., of Guthrie, Oklahoma, credited Julia Child with bringing about the change: "Through your efforts, our stores are now stocking leeks and fresh mushrooms, something unheard of 3 months ago."[29] But Julia Child wasn't solely responsible. The word spread beyond the small audience of *Gourmet* readers to the wider readership of Craig Claiborne and Jane Nickerson in the pages of the *New York Times* and on to the women's magazine audiences. Population changes brought Vietnamese, Indian, and Korean communities large enough to demand the ingredients they wanted from their local stores.

Americans, encouraged by Julia Child to have confidence in their ability to master cooking methods that went beyond opening cans and boxes, discovered the pleasures of exploring the great variety of cuisines that had, of course, been coexisting quietly in their midst. The daily necessity of fixing dinner, taking into account the likes and dislikes of family members, the budget, and the time available, did not go away, nor did the resistance of children to unfamiliar foods. But many women began to expand their horizons. Some men, encouraged by Julia Child and by later television cooking shows and intrigued by the challenge of doing something complicated, began to take an active interest in the kitchen. Cooking was no longer simply women's work.

Julia Child's classic French cooking and Grace Chu's and Joyce Chen's Chinese cooking respectfully adapted for American kitchens paved the way for Marcella Hazan's classic Italian fare. The nation's cooks came to delight in diversity—including their own. African American cookbooks took their place on the bookstore shelves: *Princess Pamela's Soul Food Cookbook*, a restaurant chef's book featuring grits and catfish stew, appeared in 1969; the delightful memoir-cookbook by Norma Jean Darden and Carole Darden, *Spoonbread and Strawberry Wine*, with recipes for chicken fricassee, fried green tomatoes, okra succotash, hush puppies and other delectable family favorites, came out in 1978. Later, the National Council of Negro Women brought out two collections, *The Black Family Reunion Cookbook* (1991) and *The Black Family Dinner Quilt Cookbook* (1993), which gather African American, West Indian, and Creole recipes along with favorite dishes that pervade the whole range of American cooking. No longer did people find it necessary to suppress the multiplicity of the countries cultural traditions; Americans were free to explore them all and enjoy the many layers that made up their diverse culinary heritage.

The enthusiasm was not universal. Many middle-class people resisted spending extra money at the supermarket to pay for exotic ingredients, and what James Beard's biographer called America's "casserole complex" did not go away. And while that tradition lingered, a new influence became visible. A decade of idealism and action, the 1960s heightened awareness. Young people working in the civil rights movement, marching against war, fighting poverty, and becoming aware of the issue of hunger, questioned the very nature of the food Americans ate. Rachel Carson's *Silent Spring* had been published in 1962; slowly but steadily, its influence spread, arousing people to the dangers of insecticides used on the farm. Respect for the environment would spread to the kitchen.

So a more sober movement began, and questions were raised about food that had nothing to do with sensual pleasure or sophisticated palates.

CHAPTER EIGHT

Brown Rice and Beans

To the many who thought that meals rich in meat, butter, milk, cheese, and cream (the best in the world, we believed) affirmed America, the land of plenty, vegetarians have seemed aberrant. They have been mocked and marginalized. Our pride in this land of plenty, however, has, throughout most of our history, coexisted with a concern for diet as one manifestation of the search for perfection, purity, and long life. Choosing to live on whole grains and fresh vegetables was not a new idea in the 1960s and 1970s.

Dr. Sylvester Graham, a notorious preacher of the gospel of wholesome diet, spread the word in the 1830s by traveling around the country giving lectures. Graham grounded his vegetarianism strictly in his view of physiology. The body, he claimed, suffered when subjected to excessive stimulation of any kind—and meat was too stimulating. His austere diet included fruits, vegetables, whole-grain cereals, and bread made with brown unsifted flour (all the bran left in) but required abstinence from meat, liquor, coffee, and tea. He also recommended daily cold baths, fresh air and exercise, and extreme moderation in sexual activity.

Dr. Graham drew a zealous following. Grahamite boardinghouses in Boston and New York promoted the diet; among their patrons were William Lloyd Garrison and other abolitionists. Enthusiasm for the movement found its way into colleges like Amherst and Williams, where small groups of students chose to dine together on

Graham bread and vegetables. For a brief time the official meal plan at Oberlin College followed the Graham diet. The students protested that they were starving. Parents complained. The Grahamite meals were abandoned, and the college community turned its moral energies toward the abolition of slavery.

Institutional programs such as those in colleges and the boardinghouses were run by men and chiefly for men. Within families, the situation was different. Disciples of Graham taught women that they could—and must—take command of their own health and raise healthy children, but also, as the historian Regina Markell Morantz puts it, that they must "[keep] their husbands moral by cooking the right foods." Morantz says, "The health reform regimen established new standards by which ordinary women could measure their own respectability and worth."[1] As women carried out the Graham program of dietary and sexual reform, household responsibilities took on a new sense of purpose and power. Cooking whole-grain cereal and baking Graham bread became evidence of women's moral superiority.

Dr. Graham retired to Northampton, Massachusetts, where he died, and his movement faded. Graham crackers are its memorial. But Graham and others succeeded in firmly planting in American nutritional culture the idea of whole grains and bran as the basis for a healthy diet. In Boston, Fannie Farmer, in 1896, differentiated between the dietary needs of sedentary professionals and those of the physical laborer. Brain workers, she cautioned (anticipating the discovery of cholesterol by decades), should not eat much meat, though fish was acceptable. Theodore Roosevelt had been a sickly child and grew up convinced of the benefits of exercise, sunshine, fresh air, a wholesome diet—and no medicine. For men, he set forth goals of building muscle and virility. But women, he declared, had a larger responsibility: "The very life and energy of the race depends upon her and her health." Women's duty was fulfilled, not by work, not by voting, but by bearing and rearing strong babies.[2]

In the 1920s and 1930s a colorful character named Bernarr Macfadden invented the phrase "physical culture" to describe his program of muscle building, vigorous exercise, and a high-fiber diet of "roughage." He advertised with pictures of his muscular self; he published a magazine, *Physical Culture*, and books with titles like *Making Old Bodies Young; The Building of Vital Power; Keeping Fit;* and *The Walking Cure: Pep and Power from Walking.* The boast of Macfadden's followers was so much a characteristic of his time that it was set to music decades later as part of the period atmosphere of *Gentlemen Prefer Blondes.* A muscular actor sang, "I start my day with a bowl of bran / And the whole day through I'm a happy man / I laugh at care and woe / I'm alive, I'm a-tingle, I'm aglow!"

By midcentury, as life expectancy increased, a new issue came to the foreground. Almost everybody liked the idea of living longer, but nobody wanted to be old or fat. The message of consolation for people who feared middle age was "life begins at forty." The star of the quest for eternal youth was Gayelord Hauser, a man described in *The New Yorker* in 1950 as "slim and immaculate," whose love of good clothes and fast cars made him a dashing figure. He prescribed a regime that included brewer's yeast, powdered skim milk, yogurt, wheat germ, and blackstrap molasses.

In earlier days, the robust body had been perceived as a healthy body; people admired fat babies, imposing men, and women with ample bosoms. Slimness was a twentieth-century ideal. Hauser united the goals of health and thinness and became famous. Celebrities adopted his spartan diet; among them were the dancer Adele Astaire, the fashionable interior decorator Elsie de Wolfe (later Lady Mendl), and the duchess of Windsor, who quipped, "You can never be too rich or too thin." Their pictures in magazines, elegantly dressed and enviably slim, set a standard that many white middle-class Americans—and others—longed to emulate. Hauser's ten- and twenty-eight day reducing diets were translated into twelve languages.

He denied being a vegetarian, but he wrote, "From the sun, air, earth and water, the green things we depend upon extract all that is good, all that is required, for health." As he vividly put it, "When you peel, pickle, cook to death, or throw away the best parts of food, you are nourishing the kitchen sink and starving your family." He condemned the use of refined white flour and worse, "Dead white sugar, probably the greatest curse in our American dietary."[3]

At the same time, Adelle Davis's books, *Let's Cook It Right* (1947),

Let's Have Healthy Children (1951), *Let's Eat Right to Keep Fit* (1954), and *Let's Get Well* (1965), were on the best-seller list. Davis, too, preached a radical change in eating habits guaranteed to win the battle against middle age and lead to energy, longevity, and youthful appearance. Scientifically trained nutritionists bemoaned her "oversimplified and at times unsound solutions to problems of nutritional deficiency," but *Time* magazine in 1972 called her "the high priestess of a new nutrition religion."[4] The combined total sales of her books and their revisions came to more than ten million copies.

While the duchess of Windsor worried about her looks, Adelle Davis urged American women to worry about their families. "It has been my purpose to show how easy cooking can be, especially for the working girl, the professional woman, and the young mother," she wrote in 1947. "These people often prepare sketchy meals because they believe cooking is difficult."[5] By 1962 she repeated this, even more strongly. With a whiff of disapproval, she remarked that "busy women often prepare sketchy and near-valueless meals because they are convinced cooking is difficult." Davis thought this was nonsense. She set out to "show how easy cooking is. There are actually only four fundamental recipes: those that tell you how to stew, fry, broil, and bake." Having mastered these techniques, she reminded her readers: "Variety lends interest to meals. A woman should be able to prepare thirty or more different entrees without repeating a menu." Davis, like her predecessors, endowed daily routine with a larger significance. "You, the homemaker," Davis stated, "are the guardian of the health of your family. If you accept this responsibility, you cannot view yourself as a kitchen drudge."[6]

Ever since the science of nutrition was discovered in the 1920s, women have worried about whether they were feeding their family the right food. Were men getting the right kind of food to support their crucial breadwinning role? Were the children getting the right vitamins so they would grow up strong and healthy? Ovaltine advertisements in the thirties warned mothers about listless, pale children suffering from secret undernourishment. Whatever theories were in fashion, the American public received its nutritional information through the pages of cookbooks and magazines aimed at women. The concern for family well-being went along with the general presumption that women took care of matters of food and diet.

A shiver of cold war anxiety crosses the pages of the 1962 edition of *Let's Cook It Right* when Davis acknowledges that among her revisions, she has added noninstant powdered milk to many recipes for extra calcium, "since radioactive fallout appears to be particularly dangerous to persons whose calcium intake is inadequate."[7] The theme of guarding the family seemed particularly appropriate to the defensive state of mind of Americans in the cold war. Many families, frightened by the prospect of nuclear war, were building private bomb shelters in their basements, stocking them with canned goods and bottled water, and arming themselves with guns they said they would use against improvident neighbors who might want to invade their bomb shelter. Magazines offered advice on stocking shelter food supplies and rotating them as their shelf life ebbed.

Home bomb shelters, extra calcium, and other cold war protective measures, in hindsight, seem pathetic. The 1982 film, *The Atomic Café*, an ironic collage of clips from newsreels and propaganda films, showed a family going into its fallout shelter, the father saying confidently, "We'll stay in here for a few hours and then everything will be all right." The next shot shows the family emerging fresh and cheerful from the shelter, with the father saying, "Now we'll just wait for the authorities to tell us what to do, and everything will be fine." This, combined with newsreel footage of Hiroshima after the bomb, provided all the comment that *The Atomic Café* needed.

Not entirely unrelated to the bomb-shelter mentality was Davis's conviction that individuals who eat the wrong food may become violent and a danger to society. She shared Hauser's view of the danger of sugar. "When the blood sugar is extremely low,the resulting irritability, nervous tension, and mental depression are such that a person can easily go berserk," she wrote in *Let's Eat Right to Keep Fit* in 1954. "If hatred, bitterness, and resentments are harbored, and perhaps a temporary psychological upset causes a person to go on a candy binge or makes it impossible for him to eat or digest food, the stage is set; violence or quarreling can occur for which there may be no forgiving. Add a few guns, gas jets, or razor blades, and you have the stuff murders and suicides are made of."[8]

But no movement for the betterment of humankind through a diet of bran and Tiger's Milk emerged. The social message—or threat—went unheeded. Davis's and Hauser's fans responded primarily to the promise of eternal youth—an appeal succinctly expressed in the promise of one of Hauser's titles, *Look Younger, Live Longer*. For this, devotees were willing to choke down daily doses of the brilliantly named but unpleasant-tasting Tiger's Milk, a concoction of skim milk, dried milk, safflower oil, vanilla, and brewer's yeast which tasted so nasty that users had to try to camouflage it with orange juice. Like blackstrap molasses, Tiger's Milk has never won anyone by its intrinsic delights.

Whether they depended on Graham bread, blackstrap molasses, bran, liver, or Tiger's Milk, these régimes were all elements of self-help programs. They promised to promote the strength and well-being—and perhaps incidentally the moral welfare—of the individual. The goal was not moral superiority but eternal youth.

––––––––

The events of the 1960s, however, led to very different concerns that formed the basis of the next major movement for healthy eating. The highly politicized decade of the civil rights and antiwar movements yielded in the mid-1970s to the politics of Watergate. Some who had been children in the fifties questioned or rejected the prevailing notions of family and many reexamined or rejected traditional standards of social behavior. The women's movement changed the expectations of women of all ages. Educated married women entered the work force in unprecedented numbers. "By the late 1960s," Stephanie Coontz writes, "for the first time, college-educated wives were *more* likely than high-school graduates to contribute financially to their families."[9] Marriage rates dropped and divorce rates rose. Many couples chose to live together before marrying, sometimes for years; some rejected the marriage ceremony altogether. When a woman did marry she was likely (in the staid phrase of the *New York Times*) to "keep her own name." Many declined to be "given away" from father to husband; they insisted on their independence.

African Americans, long disregarded by whites, became highly visible as the civil rights movement claimed national attention in the late 1950s and the 1960s. The extended family, often including members with no blood relationship, had long been a sustaining institution in that community. Now white Americans became aware of such family formations, so different from what they thought of as traditional. Diversity was replacing homogeneity. Counterculture communes expanded the definition of family. With the gay liberation movement came openly celebrated same-sex relationships. It was no longer safe to assume that that was mom bustling around in the kitchen. And whoever was stirring the pot, what simmered there might not be meat and potatoes.

A whole new vocabulary of ingredients came into the language. Tofu, miso, hummus, pita bread, foods previously known to patrons of Middle Eastern and Asian restaurants, began to appear in white middle-class kitchens. Brown rice entered the mainstream. Beans—pea beans, red beans, pinto beans, black beans—took on a new importance. They sprouted in jars covered with bits of screening and then turned up in wholesome salads and sandwiches. People kept wheat germ in the refrigerator and baked dense, healthy loaves of whole-wheat bread. Many people turned their backs not only on Boeuf Bourguignon but on hamburgers—on beef and other meats—altogether.

The diet of whole grains was certainly nothing new, but the motivation was different. The natural food movement of the seventies was based, not solely on the benefit to the individual but also on ideas about living the simple life; not only on personal betterment but also on the good of the world. Those still imbued with 1960s idealism turned from politics to an intense concern for changing social mores at home and addressing environmental and demographic concerns worldwide. By avoiding meat and manufactured foods and insisting on organic produce, people also strove to escape artificial chemical additives, pesticides, and other possibly hazardous invisible ingredients of food. They hoped to take back some control of the food supply from corporations and agribusiness. Concern about the condition of the food we eat—the standards of cleanliness, what the creatures we eat have been fed, the invisible additives—also has a long history. Progressives made it a subject of investigation and scandalous revelation at the turn of the century. The investigative reporting of Upton Sinclair and others, and the political pressure of the National Consumers' League and other consumer organizations established by women, eventually brought about the Pure Food and Drug Act of 1906 and federal meat inspection to correct or improve some of the worst offenses in food production. But by 1970 new reasons for concern existed.

Rachel Carson's *Silent Spring*, published first in *The New Yorker* and then as a best-selling book in 1962, had alerted people to the far-reaching negative effects of insecticides and food additives: chemical products that improved crop yield and made food grow larger, last longer, look fresher, or have a more appetizing color. The book had a profound impact. *Silent Spring* taught its large audience that the miraculous sprays—DDT and others—that killed off crop-threatening insects were also killing birds and animals. Over the long term, humans, too, showed ill effects. In the wake of Carson's dire warning, the miracles of modern farming looked frightening.

Coho salmon caught in Michigan turned out to be contaminated with DDT. The Food and Drug Administration ordered the recall of nearly a quarter of the canned tuna fish on the market because mercury content was above the level of safety. Cyclamate-sweetened foods were removed from the market, and baby food companies were forced to admit that monosodium glutamate could be dangerous to infants. Rodale Press's *Organic Gardening* magazine had been around since 1941, but suddenly its circulation boomed. In 1971 it had some 700,000 subscribers.[10]

If Americans were consuming poisons with their food, much of the rest of the world was simply starving. In the 1930s and 1940s, thousands of American children grew up being admonished by their mothers to clean their plates and "think of the starving children in India"—or Ethiopia or any other distant foreign land faced with famine. But now a new voice argued a direct causal relationship between the ample, meat-centered American diet and hunger in other parts of the world.

A true latter-day Progressive, Frances Moore Lappé believed that if people only knew the facts, they would not allow things to continue the way they were. Lappé has admitted to a lifelong desire to save the world. She told an interviewer in 1989 that, growing up in Fort Worth, Texas, she had dreamed of working for the State Department. A short spell at American University in Washington cooled her enthusiasm for government work. She transferred to a small Quaker college, majored in history, and went to Berkeley to study social work.

At Berkeley she became active in the movement to oppose the Vietnam war and spent her spare time helping welfare recipients organize. Concern for the world's hungry people overrode her interest in course work. She quit graduate school and began reading on her own about the political economy of food, searching for the underlying causes of the issues that troubled her. "Along with many others in the late 60's," she recalled later, "I had started out asking the question, 'how close are we to the limit of the earth's capacity to provide food for all humanity?'"[11] She became convinced that scarcity was not inevitable but instead the result of deliberate economic policies.

She undertook to educate and persuade people to a major change in eating habits, not simply for their own health or their children's but so that the food supply might be more equitably shared around the world. She dared to suggest that the American diet of meat was an inefficient use of resources. In 1971 she published *Diet for a Small Planet*, a guide to the new way of eating she recommended. She coined the phrase, "eating low on the food chain," to describe the program she advocated, by which Americans could help to stretch the world's food supply and feed the hungry.

With statistics and reasoning, Lappé made the case that the United States was wasting food resources. Then she offered an alternative to Americans' high-meat diet. The magic phrase, "complementary protein," was the key. In certain combinations, the protein in foods became more effective. When grains and legumes (beans, peas, or lentils), grains and milk products, or seeds and legumes, were combined, the sum of usable protein was greater than the parts. With texts, tables, and charts she set out to educate her readers to this new way of thinking about the structure of diet. She did not hesitate to use and explain terms like NPU ("Net Protein Utilization") or to introduce mathematical formulas. After 130 pages of explanatory text came the recipes, grouped according to the complementary items featured—rice and sesame seeds, or cornmeal and soy and milk, or wheat and beans. Fruit Pancakes sounded vaguely familiar (though hers were made with brown rice and whole-wheat flour) but Sesame-Rice Fritters? Curried Soybeans and Peanuts? These took the faith of a believer.

Lappé didn't expect people to jump into this all at once. "The notion of suddenly changing lifelong habits of any kind on the basis of new understanding does not strike me as very realistic or even desirable (however great the revelation!)," she wrote. But she was convinced that the more people understood about "the 'costliness' of meat on so many grounds" and the many interesting possibilities in the combinations she advocated, the less important meat would become in their diets.[12]

Lappé also offered her readers the promise of greater control. "Previously, when I went to a supermarket," she said in her foreword, "I felt at the mercy of our advertising culture. My tastes were manipulated. And food, instead of being my most direct link with the nurturing earth, had become mere merchandise by which I fulfilled my role as a 'good' consumer."[13]

She demanded a drastic change of diet, and found a receptive audience; by 1975 the original edition of *Diet for a Small Planet* had sold a million copies. Food became an element of a more general protest: against the consumer culture of the United States, the homogenization of everything, the promotional packaging, the corporate decisions about how we liked our soup, the assumptions about what a family was and how families lived. Against the mysterious ingredients listed on the package label in small print—hydrolized starch, xanthum gum, butylated hydroxyanisole, sodium nitrate, monosodium glutamate. And against callous indifference to the hunger of real people, real families, far away.

Young people, disaffected by the Vietnam war and disgusted with the consumer culture, turned away from the suburbs and the cities and set out to find a new kind of community in locations from

California to the pleasant hills above the Connecticut River valley in Massachusetts and Vermont. In the New England countryside land was available and they could build simple houses by hand, learning the building trades in the process. Some of them had dropped out of universities like Columbia in the stormy days of the sixties; some had degrees in physics or chemistry. Some lived alone or with a partner, some organized communes. They earned money using their self-taught skills.

Their rejection of the culture they had grown up in included a rejection of its food, the processing, the additives, the high degree of dependence on meat. They started vegetable gardens. They organized food co-ops to purchase in bulk the rice, seeds, nuts, whole-wheat flour, wheat germ, beans, and yeast that had become the basic elements of their diet.

Unlike most earlier health-food movements, this one was part of an integrated way of life and worldview. Long life, youthful physical condition, and energy were not the primary goals. These young people believed, as Lappé put it, in "food as a way to help us see our place in the world."[14]

Lappé's worldview spread to others involved in the troubled questioning of national policies of those days. For those, like me, who had learned to cook in the fifties, it was a big change. We began in a gingerly fashion, using brown rice instead of white, sneaking soy flour into our cornbread and sprinkling a little wheat germ on top of casseroles. If few of us read the entire Lappé text, we learned to mumble the mantras, "rice and legumes," "cornmeal and beans."

As Lappé's idea took hold, we tried her spinach and brown rice casserole, her Greek-Style Skillet (rice and soy grits, eggplant, green beans, tomatoes, onion and garlic with mint, dill, and parsley). But the repertoire grew like sprouts. Vegetarian restaurants sprang up in receptive college communities like Northampton, Massachusetts, and Ithaca, New York. Some of them, notably the Moosewood Restaurant and the Cabbagetown Café (both in Ithaca), became famous and eventually produced their own cookbooks, adding some needed liveliness and even glamour to vegetarian meals. In whole-food stores (many of them co-ops) barrels and bags of grains, beans, nuts, and granola, refrigerators full of tofu squares, organic cheeses, yogurt, and sprouts, and bins of unsymmetrical organically grown vegetables were accented with take-home recipes for Winter Vegetable Stew and Mediterranean Tofu-Spinach Pie.

Still, there was work to do to overcome the reputation of vegetarian cooking for dullness, for being merely "good for you." What could replace fried chicken or meat loaf? Americans were still not far from the "meat substitute" concept of World War II, with its implication of deprivation.

At first the tendency was to reproduce the format of meat-centered meals. But *The Vegetarian Epicure*, published in 1972, offered a welcome to new vegetarians and gently encouraged its readers to shake the standard meal structure along with the meat habit. The author, Anna Thomas, looked for inspiration to the cooking of Thailand, Sweden, India, and the Far East as well as the more familiar dishes of Spain and France.

It was a period of conversion; the days of certainty that a steak would please every guest were gone. For those of us who still felt the need for something that looked and tasted like a substantial main dish, Thomas's Russian Vegetable Pie, rich with cream cheese, made a reassuring company entrée. Indeed, this cookbook writer openly admitted that she intended to seduce people into appreciating vegetarian food. She heard the grumbling of the unconverted, who said, "I'd like to be a vegatarian but the food is so dull!" Her recipes were appealing and they produced delectable and even glamorous food. She did not stint on sour cream, eggs, and cheese. (She did include some recipes for nondairy vegetarians, such as Risotto Doug Edwards, a risotto made with eggplant, kidney beans, and pumpkin and sunflower seeds.) This vegetarian cookbook, like many that followed, included splendid, often rich desserts. Thomas's excuse (if anyone needed one) for these delicious concoctions—apricot mousse, cream cheese tart, or Crème Anglaise with raspberries and whipped cream—was that if the meal was low on protein, the deficiency could be made up with eggs and milk products in the dessert. (Cholesterol was not yet a familiar word.)

Neither *Diet for a Small Planet* nor *Veg Ep*, as it came to be affectionately known, addressed women in particular. But in 1976 a small publisher of "books on how to live the spiritual life in home and community" brought out a large and handsome book that soon became the Fannie Farmer of vegetarian cooking. *Laurel's Kitchen* is a comprehensive guide to vegetarian food. Its author, Carol Flinders, like her mentor, Laurel Robertson, regarded a vegetarian diet as an integral part of a way of life she described as "living intentionally." She placed the responsibility for adopting this life directly in the hands of women.

Women, she said, taking her cue from Lappé, "have a vital role to play in steering our small planet out of its present disaster course." No longer was it enough for a woman to feed her husband and children nourishing meals. "For the rest of this century," she announced, "the American housewife is in a uniquely important role. As never before, the 'gift of life' is hers to give or withhold." Reminding her readers that traditionally, "it was the woman's wise allocation of limited supplies that would see the family through," she added, "now we need to become trustees not just for our immediate families, but for the entire planet." [15]

In this small world, however, home and neighborhood provided "the most effective front for social change." Her general recommendation sounded simple. "In summary, our advice goes like this: eat a good variety of whole, fresh, natural foods (vegetarian, of course) that are cooked with love and taken in temperate quantity." [16]

The person who "cooked with love" and tended to the supply of food was a woman. She stayed at home so that she would have time to bake bread and make Better Butter, an alternative to margarine that was a combination of safflower oil, butter, water and dried skim milk with a little lecithin and salt. She packed wholesome lunches for her husband and children to take to school and work, and they were not simple. She included homemade soup or chilled steamed vegetables with salad dressing, sandwiches of peanut butter and chopped dates or split-pea-and-Parmesan spread, and fresh fruit.

"You will look in vain in our book for a section on time-saving tips, for one of our firmest beliefs is that we Americans wouldn't be in the pickle we're in today were it not for our burning desire to *save time* at any cost. So be prepared to spend more time in the kitchen than you might be used to,"[17] warned the introduction to the recipes section of the book.

If brown rice and beans were the mainstays of the responsible meal plan, bread was the keystone of the intentional life. *Diet for a Small Planet* stressed the value of grains, but Frances Moore Lappé was hardly a homebody. Her book included some recipes for pancakes, waffles, and muffins (all made from a basic quick mix of whole-wheat and soy flours, baking powder, dry milk, wheat germ, and salt), and one all-purpose Wheat-Soy-Sesame Bread.

But bread suited the domestic life prescribed by *Laurel's Kitchen* perfectly. The first time Carol Flinders met her idol, Laurel Robertson, she was "just setting out four long, fat strips of dough to rise for French bread." This bread, along with homemade soup, could supply energy to a meeting of protesters against the Vietnam war. Laurel, Flinders observed with awe, "was right out of Vermeer—a sturdy young woman in her early twenties with wide, clear blue eyes and a thick braid, her sleeves rolled up, a vast white apron over her long skirts." Besides cooking wholesome food in her sunny kitchen filled with potted plants, Laurel held two part-time jobs, did calligraphy for good causes, and had been arrested during a protest demonstration.[18]

Flinders's description of her first visit to an organic food co-op has eery echoes of Edward Bellamy's utopian novel, *Looking Backward*, published in 1888. When Bellamy's narrator, having fallen asleep in Boston in 1887, wakes to find himself in a socialist Utopia of the year 2000, he marvels at the "stalwart young men and fresh, vigorous maidens." Similarly, Flinders's "stomach sank" when she entered the food co-op. "Moving about me confidently on every side were lithe, tawny young men and women in faded blue denims, peasant blouses, and skirts made from old bedspreads, their thick manes braided, rubber-banded, or falling free."[19] Laurel appears, as if by magic, like Bellamy's benevolent host Dr. Leete, to be her guide. And in due course, Laurel teaches her to make bread.

The sensual, back-to-nature feel of making bread is certainly one of its charms. On the practical side, homemade bread was the stealth weapon of the new complementary protein diet; a good loaf of bread made with whole-wheat flour and wheat germ could also conceal soy flour and soy grits (thus combining complementary beans and wheat) and could be made more delicious as well as more nourishing by including sunflower or sesame seeds, nuts, and dried fruit.

But bread also made a good symbol for the creativity that cooking, approached in the right way, could unleash. The poet Bethami Auerbach, in "The Search for the Perfect Rye Bread," defends the hours she has spent making bread. For a writer, "these are hours / when something is going on in my life, / hours when I might be home / staring at my hands / in terror that nothing is going on in my life." And in fact, sometimes the hours produce more than a loaf of bread: ". . . after washing my spoon, / I might grab my pen; / hours of waiting / for a sign / that I can make something / out of nothing." A lawyer for the Environmental Protection Agency, Auerbach says in a headnote to the poem, "Sometimes I can finish a poem on a weekend while I'm waiting for my bread to come out of the oven."[20]

If Charlotte Perkins Gilman had sought escape from the kitchen, Carol Flinders might have appeared to seek escape *to* the kitchen, out of a world that had become scary and stressful. Resisting mass production and its additives meant returning production—of bread and many other things—to the home kitchen. Mason jars covered with cheesecloth or window screening lay on their sides in kitchens, with little gardens of sprouts—alfalfa, mung bean, lentil or soy—growing inside. They required watering three times a day. In other jars, bathed in warm water or sitting on a heating pad, or in a special electric yogurt maker, yogurt developed. Weekends spent growing sprouts and yogurt, kneading bread and making soup yielded a pleasant feeling of accomplishment.

In contrast to the precise recipes, nutritional charts, and plans for preparing stocks of wholesome food that characterize *Laurel's Kitchen*, *Tassajara Cooking*, a cookbook from the Zen Mountain Center where students of Zen Buddhism lived and, in summer, welcomed guests, expressed a simple philosophy. "Begin and continue with what is in front of you," advised the author, Edward Brown. "The way to be a cook is to cook. . . . Our cooking doesn't have to prove how wonderful or talented we are." The spiritual foundation of Zen imbues the book. The practice at the Zen Center, where anything not grown there must be carried up a long mountain road, is to use what is there. The book begins with a careful description of the art of using a knife for cutting vegetables. "Cut steadily, evenly, rhythmically, letting speed come with practice," it advises.[21]

Often the recipes simply list possible ingredients: potatoes, carrots, onion, water, salt, for example (quantities are not specified) to be combined and steamed or baked. A dish with a name that suggests an abstract painting, "Orange & Green on White," combines boiled cauliflower, grated Cheddar cheese, and chopped green onion or parsley. The emphasis is on "preparing things so that we can enjoy their unique spirit."[22]

The natural food movement had considerable permanent effect. On my own pantry shelves today I have Mason jars filled with brown rice, kasha, bulgur, black beans, white beans, pinto beans, anasazi beans, sunflower seeds, and sesame seeds. In 1970 I had never heard of most of these items. Now they are staples. Marion Rombauer Becker, who had long had a personal interest in the environment and in healthful eating, realized when she prepared the 1975 edition of *The Joy of Cooking* that many of her readers shared her interest. "She was emboldened to direct *Joy* more emphatically to issues that she had first noticed decades before," Anne Mendelson writes, "the impoverishment of soil through overexploitation or crude dosing with chemical fertilizers, the troubling environmental repercussions of 'chickens fed in batteries, pigs and cattle concentrated in feed lots,'" water and air pollution.[23]

It's true that after a while, in most households, the yogurt maker and the sprouting jars worked their way to the farthest corner of the kitchen cupboard. Home production no longer was necessary. A variety of yogurts and sprouts appeared even in the supermarket. Wholegrain bread and granola became more generally available. And after all, many of us who had recently emerged from 1950s housewifery to belated starts in careers were not prepared to accept the exhortations of *Laurel's Kitchen* and try another version of domesticity as life work. Indeed, more than one feminist has argued that *Laurel's Kitchen* set back the women's movement.

Many food co-ops met the same fate as the dining co-ops had

earlier: differences among the members and declining enthusiasm caused their demise. But some survived, and from the ranks of cooperators came entrepreneurs who established small stores specializing in selling beans, nuts, and grains from barrels, tofu, freshly ground peanut butter, and organically grown vegetables.

The food industry fought back, claiming it was only trying to defend a naive public against "food radicals." But then, when its own surveys and studies showed that better-off consumers were interested in "natural" foods and concerned about nutrition, it recognized a market. Poor people and people who had been poor might insist on "the culinary symbols of affluence," meat, refined flour, sugar. "While affluent people could afford more of these emblems, they took them more for granted and were perhaps more secure in cutting back voluntarily," Warren J. Belasco says. Marketers decided the future lay with the elite "opinion leaders." Corporations seized on the language of the whole-food movement and began sprinkling the word "natural" through their advertising and developing names for their products that suggested old-fashioned virtues. But as Belasco points out, "the actual content of mass-marketed natural foods could be as vague as the word itself." Even Velveeta cheese was described by the manufacturer as "a blend of natural cheeses." Granola, the basic food of the counterculture, entered the mainstream in 1973 when companies like Quaker Oats and Kellogg introduced their own brand-name versions.[24]

The concern for all the people of the planet that had motivated many to adopt at least part of the counterculture's diet began to give way to the quest for individual fulfillment—"doing your own thing." Meanwhile, scientific research highlighted a hazard to long life: cholesterol. The interest in vegetarian recipes found a new motivation. The discovery of the evils of cholesterol led many people who were not vegetarian from principle to look for low-fat food and alternatives to meat. Many Americans still loved a good roast beef dinner, but became sadder and wiser; they noticed that far away, people who of necessity subsist mainly on rice and other grains and vegetables may live longer.

Vegetarian cookbooks multiplied. Cholesterol and salt joined chemicals as hidden risks of food. Butter became a villain. The great

American breakfast, fried eggs and bacon, turned out to be hazardous. A great transformation of eating habits took place as people adopted low-fat diets from medical necessity or fear.

The immediate reaction of many people whose doctors told them that high cholesterol counts posed a threat to their lives was despair. Give up steak, cheese, butter? Cut down on eggs? Life would be drab indeed. The first "heart-healthy," low-cholesterol, low-salt cookbooks were, indeed, quite spartan. Once again, we needed an authoritative and imaginative text. Jane Brody, a science and medical writer for the *New York Times*, stepped in. As Pierre Franey, well known for his love of fine food and his excellent recipes, put it, "Just after she has informed us that practically every evident tendency in American eating is misdirected—too much fat, too much protein, too much sugar, and too much salt—she manages to persuade us that life can still be worth living."[25] First came *Jane Brody's Nutrition Book* in 1981, a manual of nutritional advice with some recipes. Then came a television series and a thorough cookbook, *Jane Brody's Good Food Book*, published in 1985.

Brody had learned to cook by "reading and watching, but mostly through trial and error."[26] She was no spartan; she clearly enjoyed cooking and eating. Like Rombauer, she adopted the conversational tone of a friend sharing recipes, but her recipes were backed by an impressive scientific knowledge. Like Lappé, she had first to educate her audience to a new vocabulary of ingredients and a new way of thinking about food. She devoted a third of the book to an encyclopedic text on the nutritional values and hazards of various foods and an introduction to some unfamiliar, but useful, ingredients such as millet and buckwheat.

The key to Brody's appeal is that she did not demand abandoning familiar favorites. Instead, she adjusted them to fit dietary limitations. Her approach to eggs, for example, was not to rule them out entirely, but to alter recipes so they included only half as many yolks as whites. She was among the first to advocate thinking of meat "as an ingredient rather than the featured item in a dish," and to urge people to stop "basing a meal around a hunk of meat."[27] Her vegetarian recipes show the influence of Lappé and the complementary protein idea.

As a parent "who raised two normally picky eaters," she was sympathetic to the problems of readjusting a family's food habits.

In the nineties, healthy eating became an obsession. Magazines thrived on it, for example, *Eating Light, Vegetarian Times*, and *Cooking Light*. Translations of old-fashioned recipes to versions acceptable to the "healthy cook" appeared daily. Perhaps one of the most unexpected was Roy F. Guste Jr.'s *Louisiana Light* (1990), which skillfully adapted the rich fare of Cajun cooking to a reasonably low-fat diet.

One day I picked up a copy of *Woman's Day* and found a recipe called "Mom's Casserole for the '90s." I recognized it, but it was like meeting an old friend who has lost a lot of weight, much changed but still recognizable. My old favorite from years back had been a rich concoction of noodles, ground chuck, tomato sauce, a half pound each of cottage cheese and cream cheese, and sour cream, enhanced with scallions, a tablespoon of green pepper, and melted butter. It was a classic—Gertrude May had her own version of it on Iowa radio in the 1930s. But the sadder but wiser cook of the nineties would have shuddered at the thought. In the 1990s, noodles were a variety of pasta (a term that wasn't part of our language earlier in the century), now a much-respected "complex carbohydrate." Ground turkey replaced ground chuck. Low-fat tomato soup replaced the tomato sauce. Nonfat cottage cheese substituted for the cheeses and sour cream of the original. And broccoli, the mighty fighter against disease, was smuggled in to do its good work. This version is wholesome, low-cholesterol, low-fat, and low-calorie, and it won't give you a heart attack.

A lot of people have changed their diets considerably and some have become vegetarians, but the message of *Diet for a Small Planet* has largely been forgotten. If people eat beans, nuts, and grains today it is generally for the sake of their own health; few think of any possible effect on world hunger. With the close of the 1970s, the generous American enterprise of modifying eating patterns in order to share food more equably around the world gradually lost currency. The language of the whole earth gave way to that of self-help and self-interest, and conspicuous consumption achieved heights that would have astonished Thorstein Veblen, the man who, in 1899, coined the phrase.

CHAPTER NINE

The New American Cuisine at Home

IN THE AFFLUENT EIGHTIES, THE MOST NOTICEABLE AUTHORS OF NEW COOKBOOKS WERE NOT PRACTICAL IDEALISTS; NOR were they old-fashioned neighborly sharers of cooking secrets or teachers instructing students in the basics. From San Francisco to Boston, restaurants had emerged that were celebrated for their new American cooking—a cuisine that emphasized fresh ingredients and inventiveness. As the nation prospered, well-off diners enjoyed the pleasures of these often expensive restaurants, while others read about them in food magazines or newspapers and wished they were there. The chefs knew the cooking of France and Italy, of Thailand and Japan, but instead of imitating, they drew on them to develop a style of their own. Some of these young chefs were offspring of the counterculture, attentive to environment, farming practices, and political issues. Julia Child's success had demonstrated that there was a market for ambitious cookbooks, and now sophisticated restaurant cooks became an important influence on home cooking.

Famous chefs, from the fabled Escoffier to the mid-twentieth century's Louis de Gouy, have shared their secrets in cookbooks before. But in the late years of the twentieth century, an audience educated by *Gourmet* and *Bon Appetit* and the food pages of the *New York Times*—to say nothing of Julia Child's television teaching—was eager to learn the tricks of the trade, and a wave of glamorous cookbooks appeared.

An early leader in the field was Alice Waters. Her restaurant, Chez Panisse, opened in Berkeley, California, in 1971 with a five-course, fixed-price menu that changed daily, offering the highest quality products available that day. Waters had traveled and studied in France after graduating from Berkeley; she was inspired not only by the fine cooking of France but also by the neighborhood markets with their abundance of fresh produce, local cheeses, and excellent meat and fish. Living in Berkeley, she surely learned the consciousness of freshness and purity of ingredients that developed in the counterculture and is a characteristic of *Laurel's Kitchen.*

The menus at Chez Panisse rely on daily visits to the richly stocked markets; the staff now includes a person whose job title is "forager," someone who searches out producers of the best ingredients. Preferring to buy locally grown produce, along with the freshest fish and the very best of meat, Waters and her staff began encouraging farmers and ranchers in the area who followed organic methods. This did not mean they were limited to standard United States farm products. When they wanted something not usually available here, they coaxed farmers into growing it. Farmers around Berkeley began producing a wide variety of greens, miniature potatoes, tiny carrots, and jewel-like beets; dairies were persuaded to produce fresh goat cheese and crème fraîche. Waters and her staff introduced new ingredients into their cooking and, as other restaurants and cooks at home picked up their ideas, created a larger market for them. The Chez Panisse idea of shopping is a far cry from going to the supermarket with a list and coming home with a pound of hamburger, cans of tomato and mushroom soup, and iceberg lettuce, but over time, Waters's and other chefs' marketing lists have influenced the vast increase in once-exotic foods that are available in today's supermarkets.

Waters and other cooks who came of age in the seventies and eighties based their style on an array of ingredients from a wide variety of sources—fresh cilantro, Hungarian paprika, Asian spices, red, yellow, purple, and green peppers of various degrees of heat. And many of them wrote books to show the home cook how she or he could achieve similar results. Waters believes in buying from local producers and in encouraging people to grow their own (she has been involved in a public school project growing food for the school cafeteria in Berkeley and launched a prison garden project in San Francisco) but her main interest is clear: "I opened a restaurant so that everybody could come and eat," she writes in the introduction to her *Chez Panisse Menu Cookbook*. "Remember that the final goal is to nourish and nurture those who gather at your table. It is there, within this nurturing process, that I have found the greatest satisfaction and accomplishment."[1] The spirit is appealing, though to gather at the Chez Panisse table diners must be well-heeled and have made reservations far in advance. For others, the cookbook may offer an approximation.

Julee Rosso and Sheila Lukins began their food careers, not as restaurant chefs but as the cook-owners of a gourmet food shop, the Silver Palate, in New York City. Recognizing from their own experience the need for some relief in the endless juggling of schedules and activities, they planned "a tiny gem of a shop where the best foodstuffs could be available" to take away, serving families and single people who wanted to entertain or just to have something good for dinner. Inspired by the shop's huge success, in 1979 they published their first book of recipes, *The Silver Palate Cookbook*.

The book, not surprisingly, offered many recipes for the very kind of elegant appetizers and salads that characterized the shop. The emphasis was on parties and the recipes ambitious. Far from Manhattan, a cook could concoct miniature quiches filled with Peppers Provençal; with patience and clever hands, she could create New Potatoes with Black Caviar. Even hikers could eat well; a delectable back-packing picnic menu included Chicken Liver Paté with Green Peppercorns, assorted sausages, and Brie cheese, as well as Tomato, Montrachet and Basil Salad, French bread, grapes and strawberries, and Shortbread Hearts.

After the success of *The Silver Palate* and its sequel, *The Silver Palate Good Times Cookbook* (1984), Lukins and Rosso moved on to a major undertaking, *The New Basics Cookbook*. This book went beyond gourmet catering food; its nearly 850 pages included a pantry list, a glossary, and other technical information. It clearly set out to replace Fannie Farmer or *The Joy of Cooking* as a comprehensive guide for the late-twentieth-century cook.

The women of Napton, who through the long winters depended on fruits and vegetables they had preserved during the summer and fall, would be astonished to learn that this cookbook was inspired by "the vast cornucopia of ethnic, exotic, and regional cuisines." In the world of *New Basics* the kitchen always has "vegetable crispers . . . packed with lush greens, peppers, beets, and eggplants in a rainbow of colors. There are always tomatoes ripening to perfection for a quick bruschetta, fresh or dried wild mushrooms to turn into a glorious risotto or pasta sauce, and pesto to spread on crostini."[2] To paraphrase Dorothy's wondering line at the moment when *The Wizard of Oz* changes from black and white to color, this wasn't Missouri.

The mentors have changed. Fannie Farmer was a teacher. Irma Rombauer was the surrogate mother (or perhaps the skilled and good-humored neighbor) who shared her cooking secrets and knew absolutely everything. Even "The French Chef," Julia Child, who had learned classic French cooking from experts so she could practice it at home, saw herself as a home-kitchen teacher. But now cookbook authors were professional cooks. For the cook at home, a recent cookbook or the latest issue of *Gourmet, Saveur, Bon Appétit*, or some newer food magazine in hand, these chef-instructors have given cooking a very different look, placing a high value on sophistication and the novelty of imaginative cooking. Alluring writing and often delectable illustration inspire their readers. Complex, detailed recipes found an appreciative audience among those who would like to be equally imaginative and daring—or who enjoy reading about people who are—but by their example they also encouraged experimentation. Docility and dogged obedience to scientific rules went out when Julia Child came in. The chefs' recipes can be followed exactly, but they can also be adjusted, experimented with, or used as inspiration for something different. A brochure promoting a new magazine called *Fine Cooking* in the summer of 1996 promised, "Something we won't do is preach to you about what you ought to cook." Persuasion, not preaching, was the way to lure people into their kitchens as the century approached its end.

The mentors of earlier years, many of them trained as home economists and nutritionists, took the hands of fledgling cooks (as mothers and aunts once did) and showed them how to cope with the day-in, day-out need to feed a family or give a party. Their basic assumption was that a woman cooked to feed her family. The new mentors, professional cooks and experts at entertaining people with food, were more like the tennis coaches who help average athletes come closer to the dream of playing a brilliant game. Pleasing others was no longer necessarily the primary motive. The busy culture demanded that if a woman or man spend time cooking, the activity itself must be entertaining. The self insisted on first consideration. Cooking is a form of self-expression that is ready at hand; the cook seeks pleasure in the kitchen. If the results also please others, that's a bonus.

Julia Child helped people brave the mysteries of French cooking and began the challenge to more ambitious work in the kitchen. The sixties, as we have seen, brought a rush of cautious experimentation with a wider variety of cuisines. Marcella Hazan in two large volumes, *The Classic Italian Cookbook* (1980) and *More Classic Italian Cooking* (1982) splendidly taught the simple, perfect secrets of Italian cooking. These cooking mentors wielded their influence by way of television as well as books and magazines; they created desires with their recipes, their pantry lists, their elegantly photographed presentations, and their enthusiasm for emulating great cuisine.

But the chefs' cookbooks taught a different approach. The original style of the New American Cuisine, with a rich multicultural vocabulary of ingredients and cooking methods, appealed to the sophisticated Americans who cooked, probably not on a daily basis, but in their leisure time, for the joy of it.

Under the chefs' influence, the grocery store changed, too. Produce sections have expanded. It's not enough that avocados are almost always available; shoppers also expect mangos and papayas and of course the now ubiquitous kiwi fruit. Nevertheless, the image, designed in California and nurtured by restaurateurs, of perfectly fresh, recently picked vegetables and fruits must remain, for most of the year, something of an unattainable ideal for the many Americans living in the harsher climates of New England or the Midwest. The supermarkets rely on cheap imports and modern shipping speed to provide peaches, melons, and asparagus as well as more exotic fruits and vegetables; in the nineties, Americans began to realize that there was little or no control over the working conditions and pay of the people who grew and picked them, or regulation of the use of pesticides and chemical fertilizers. As the decade drew to a close, movements to encourage local producers were born.

The variety of available ingredients did increase amazingly, first in urban areas, gradually spreading to farther reaches. Rosso and Lukins note that when they opened their shop, shallots were hard to find; even in Manhattan, they had only one supplier. Now shallots are plentiful in many supermarkets. While I lived in a western New England college town, in the seventies, I witnessed a transformation in food shopping. In spaces that had once housed a small-city department store, a hardware store, or a hairdressing establishment, specialty food shops appeared. A shop that sold serious coffee beans and coffee-making equipment opened; a bakery that produced wonderful European-style bread appeared. Exploring, somebody discovered a Portuguese butcher and an excellent wine store in the old town of Ludlow a few miles away. A Saturday visit to the Italian neighborhood in Springfield could provide us with fresh tortellini, prosciutto, provolone, black olives, and other delights the supermarkets didn't stock. Thanks to local orchards, we had apples in great variety. But the New England climate didn't change; fresh, flavorful tomatoes were available for only a few weeks in late summer.

Thanks to the Connecticut River flood plain, we feasted each spring on locally grown, freshly picked asparagus, eating it nearly every day of its all-too-brief season. We ate it plain, steamed, with butter and lemon; we gently placed a poached egg on top of a pile of green stalks for breakfast; we served it cold with a vinaigrette for lunch; it became the centerpiece of spring dinners. I seldom bothered to make Hollandaise. My grandmother would have been disappointed in me, but the thin stalks were so delicious it seemed like gilding the lily.

Then in 1986 we moved to Georgia. To my northern eye, the supermarket offerings seemed prosaic. For a long time, each visit back north would find me returning with a big shopping bag full of bread and coffee. In time, I discovered alternatives, like the giant DeKalb Farmers' Market on the outskirts of Atlanta. I learned to enjoy greens and grits, and I improved my skill at making biscuits, though they are still too large. (A southern woman once told me, "A lady is known by the size of her biscuits—the smaller the biscuit, the more ladylike the lady.")

Whatever part of the country you live in, if you want to cook like Alice Waters or the Silver Palate duo, clearly you will want to forget stocking the pantry with cans of tuna fish and boxes of macaroni, with catsup, baked beans, and canned mushrooms, as Fannie Farmer and Irma Rombauer recommended. Instead, the shelves must be filled with a dazzling array of exotic ingredients. *Good and Plenty*, published in 1988 by two Chez Panisse alumnae, included on its supply list arrowroot and baking powder (familiar to Fannie Farmer) but also capers, dried chili peppers, sesame oil, artichoke hearts, and roasted red peppers.[3] *The New Basics*, with its New York specialty food shop background, suggested chile oil, hoisin sauce, sun-dried tomatoes packed in oil, canned escargots, a wardrobe of vinegars including, of course, balsamic, and water chestnuts, along with four kinds of rice and eight of dried pasta. In order to take advantage of the *New York Times*'s helpful and frequent advice on fast ten-minute dinners, it helped to keep a pantry inventory that included five kinds of canned beans, instant couscous, polenta, anchovies, chutneys, and a selection of salsas. Cumin, coriander, and cardamom joined cinnamon and cloves as essentials of the spice shelf. It was exciting to have these ingredients at your disposal, but it added considerably to the checkout-counter total.

Although their recipes and pantry lists hardly evoke the farm cooking of earlier days, the authors of these cookbooks claimed simplicity of outlook. "After being caught up in a whirlwind the past twenty years," the authors of *The New Basics* told their readers, "with food fads and lifestyles changing faster than you can run a marathon, many people say that it is now time to take a breath, slow down, and hark back to a simpler time in America."[4] This meant meat loaf, for example, but none of the four recipes was ordinary. One was a Cajun version, one devised by a chef at a Venice, California, restaurant; a complicated "subtle yet complex" version had three layers, each a different mixture; the simplest was made with herbs and a layer of sliced hard-boiled eggs. There have always been many ways to prepare meat loaf (in fact, the hard-boiled egg trick isn't new), but few were as adventurous as these. The *New Basics*'s authors were gazing at the simpler time through a prism of sophisticated taste.

In the celebrity-driven atmosphere of the nineties, the role of old-fashioned neighborly adviser might be said to have been filled by Martha Stewart, not a professional cook but the professional Perfect Housewife. No area of the house and garden escaped her attention. In her magazine, *Martha Stewart Living*, and her television program, of the same name, and in her numerous books about gardening, decorating, and cooking she raised expectations to a level impossible for most people to achieve. She drew strong positive and negative response. Like the home economics experts, she turned housekeeping into a professional task; unlike her predecessors, she addressed an audience largely composed of women who were already pursuing one career. Working women have always been expected to come home and do the cooking and housework, but this was the double day carried to new heights.

Martha Stewart's Quick Cook, published in 1983, and its sequel, *Martha Stewart's Quick Cook Menus*, originated, she tells us, "when I was a stockbroker on Wall Street" with a young daughter and a lawyer husband. This was a far remove from the political world of *Diet for a Small Planet* and *Laurel's Kitchen*. Stewart invented these meals for herself to cook after she arrived home from work at five or six o'clock; preparation time was limited to an hour or less. Pierre Franey's *The Sixty-Minute Gourmet* and many other books focus on fixing good food in a short time, but this was Martha Stewart, so it was not quite that simple. Among the goals she set for herself were "to create mouth-watering, nutritious, healthful meals in a matter of minutes" and "to set a lovely, unusual table in a very short time."[5] She shopped at the greengrocer, the fishmonger, the cheese store, the bakery. A typical meal includes pan-sautéed trout, homemade fresh red pepper pasta (she confesses that she likes to make this ahead and freeze it), an endive and radicchio salad. But the recipes are not all. Presentation must be attended to with care and precision; for instance, she is fond of tying bundles of food (green beans, for example) in ribbons made of strips of steamed leek. (Remember Fannie Farmer's Berkshire Salad in Boxes?) The captions for the book's gorgeous color photographs explain that each dish is cooked and/or served in a special antique dish—an oval copper pan for the trout, for example, or Quimperware bowls for the soup, or some other utensil from the apparently vast collection she has gathered on her travels. Everything is in perfect taste.

All this elegance was seductive. Even a reader who intended only to adopt one idea or recipe could be driven to anxiety and doubt by Stewart's adamant suggestions and minute attention to detail. Shouldn't the table be set with monogrammed linen napkins (ironed, of course)? Do I dare to eat a pear if I don't caramelize it first? With Stewart, the ancient art of preparing food for survival and the sustaining of human values had given way to something suspiciously like Veblen's conspicuous consumption.

Technological developments in the kitchen, promoted as time-saving tools to make easy meal preparation even easier, also have supported more ambitious home cooking. Even the back-to-basics rhetoric of the comfort-food school did not suggest whisking away the convenient products of technology that line the counters of contemporary kitchens.

Middle-class women have not lost their kitchens, as Charlotte Perkins Gilman hoped and predicted as the century opened; instead, they gained an array of electric outlets. Technology mushroomed. Where once only the toaster had to be plugged in, by the nineties kitchen counters might boast a food processor, a blender, a mixer (at least a hand mixer), a coffee maker, possibly a bread machine and a pasta maker, and more—as well as one appliance predicted by the visionaries of the 1950s that actually made it into real life, the microwave oven.

Once the peddler came to the farmhouse in Napton, Missouri, with a wagon full of gadgets designed by clever inventors to ease the housewife's chores. The peddler was replaced by the mail carrier, bringing glossy catalogs to peddle a myriad of kitchen tools. Some of the gadgets hadn't changed much: with more than a touch of nostalgia in its catalog copy, the Vermont Country Store will sell you a crank-operated flour sifter or an old-fashioned slotted potato masher just like the ones the peddlers carried, as well as the latest in a long line of human-powered apple parers. But in addition, from Williams Sonoma, the Chef's Catalog, and numerous others comes an endless proliferation of electric grinders, mixers, juicers, pasta makers, rice cookers, bread machines, ice cream makers and other single-purpose machines to crowd kitchen counters and occupy banks of electrical outlets.

The food processor (a French invention) pushed the blender into the corner. Many cooks praised it as their indispensable sous-chef, swiftly coping with mundane tasks of chopping, slicing, and puréeing, making julienne vegetables in seconds, and even mixing pastry dough to perfection. The cook who failed to achieve a Zen-like level of contemplation while chopping was delighted to let the machine mince onions. Like other appliances before it, it came bearing promises to lessen drudgery, but could lure a cook who once was satisfied with quick and simple dishes into undreamed-of complexities. There it sat, occupying a large swatch of counter space, demanding to be used. Suddenly homemade mayonnaise seemed like a good idea, then it was on to aioli. I held out against owning a food processor for years; I really enjoy the task of chopping and mincing with a good knife and my blender took care of purées. Eventually the smell of my old blender motor's overheating in its valiant effort to turn chick peas and sesame paste into hummus drove me to it. I have had to admit that, even with all its parts elbowing the dishes out of the way in the dishwasher, it's a valued ally.

The food processor is a tool for the person who enjoys cooking; people who don't like to cook wouldn't perform its tricks anyway. The microwave, on the other hand, exists mainly to fulfill the dreams of those who wish they didn't have to cook at all. Lots of microwave owners sheepishly confess to using this technological wonder only to heat up a cup of coffee, warm the baby's bottle, or reheat doggie-bag food from Chinese restaurants. But even the microwave has its gourmet supporters. The food writer Barbara Kafka published two enormous collections of delectable recipes for the microwave; a whole meal on a plate can be produced in moments and there are no pots and pans to wash. Julie Sahni devised an array of Indian dishes to cook in the microwave. But however delicious the product, the microwave separates the cook from the sensual pleasure of the doing; there's no peeking, no stirring up, no tasting, no sniffing appetite-enhancing scents.

The bread machine invites an even more vigorous quarrel between technology and the cook's own hands. The ability to make and serve and eat homemade bread, every day if the baker wants, is certainly desirable. A fresh warm loaf ready for dinner is, of course, an appetizing idea. But a powerful attraction is the physical control of the bread's ingredients. A good many people buy bread machines because they are suspicious of the unpronounceable ingredients listed on the wrappers of factory-made bread. They're not interested in the art of baking. For health reasons they want to know exactly what goes into their bread. The machine makes this easy.

But if, like me, you love to dig your hands into the dough and knead, to feel it change and grow under your fingers, to punch it down and make the expanded ball sink, to shape it and watch it rise again, then the attraction of the bread machine is faint.

The homely pressure cooker, an old dog that few people have ever loved, has seen another attempted renaissance. Practical home economists of the twenties and the forties extolled its virtues, almost begging cooks to use their pressure cookers, for efficiency and for preserving vitamins. The earth-friendly diet of the seventies with its emphasis on dried beans made the pressure cooker seem a convenient alternative to hours of cooking. More recently, it has been recommended for people who like to cook at home but have little time to get dinner on the table. It all makes perfect sense, but the pressure cooker has never become very popular. Lorna J. Sass, an enthusiastic pressure-cooker advocate, lamented in 1989 that "by the late fifties, some 45 million pressure cookers were unaccountably stowed away in attics and forgotten."[6] Attempting a revival, she filled her cookbook with exotic dishes, but the attic is still home to many a pressure cooker.

Why have so many cooks resisted? The pressure cooker has always suffered from a reputation for danger of explosions or steam burns. Manufacturers have worked hard to overcome the bad press that stemmed from accidents with early designs. But more than that, its defect, like that of the microwave and the bread machine, is that it does its work in secret. The cook can't intervene until it's all done and the lid has been gingerly removed. Consider, for example, a pressure-cooked risotto recipe that appeared in *Cook's Magazine* in 1996. On the one hand, if you really love to eat risotto, this is a method of cooking it that doesn't require standing at the stove for half an hour, stirring. On the other hand, if cooking risotto gives you even more pleasure than eating it, then you might be happy to stand over an ordinary pot, judiciously adding small amounts of stock and watching the grains of rice gently swell.

People who aimed to cook like restaurant chefs inevitably attracted the attention of marketers who set out to convince them that they needed restaurant-quality equipment. For people who wanted to show their "professional" style, and could afford it, designer lines of expensive, chef-quality, name-brand, heavy stainless steel or anodized aluminum saucepans or sauté pans appeared. They stood ready to take their places on a powerful gas stove designed for a restaurant, large and impressive enough to stand up to the old iron range of Mrs. Abney's day, and far more expensive. Home cooks who took to cooking like chefs acquired equipment to match their ambitions.

We did not arrive at the state that David Sarnoff, the vigorously outspoken advocate of technology who was head of RCA, predicted in 1955, when he said, "Small atomic generators, installed in homes and industrial plants, will provide power for years and ultimately for a lifetime without recharging."[7] The robot servants some people expected have not shown up at the door. These wonders didn't come to pass, but grocery shopping services on the Web approximated the push-button shopping once anticipated. Inventors dream up occasional schemes for feeding recipes into a computer that will then take care of the cooking. But in most households, a human consciousness still decides what's for dinner and sees that it arrives at the table.

The home kitchen, so handsomely equipped, once again became the center of the house. Architectural design, responding to wealthy customers' preference, favored large spaces that combine the functions of family room, dining space, and kitchen in enormous houses with vestigial living rooms. Many of the people who enjoy cooking creatively also enjoy cooking in public. The kitchen became, for them, a theater. The thought that kitchen work should be invisible vanished. At the end of a work day, or on a Sunday evening, they invited their friends into the kitchen to watch and talk while they cook. The style promoted by the new American cuisine invented by restaurant chefs requires that many dishes—the risotto, the pasta with fresh vegetables, the Goat Cheese Soufflé—be attended to frequently while they are cooking and be served at once. Everything is in the open, the guests are in their places, and the food is presented with a flourish. Cooking becomes performance art.

Running against the tide of both sophisticated and heart-healthy cuisine, in the mid-1990s came another trend, a nostalgic, defiant resurrection of the fondly remembered old-fashioned food of home and diner: meat loaf, macaroni and cheese, even cherry pie. The comfort food remembered from a fifties childhood found a place in the pages of *Gourmet* magazine: Jane and Michael Stern reported on restaurants where old-fashioned pot roast with gravy and mashed potatoes with lots of butter can be found along with hot dogs and baked ham. In uncertain times, perhaps some people look for reassurance in food favorites from their nursery.

Cooking, no longer essential as it was in Napton, has had a bewildering array of identities. In the last years of the century, it became a challenge for overachievers and an area of competition for people who had become accustomed to constant striving at work or play. If cooking is not necessary it can be made complicated enough to provide intense challenge. Julia Child's approach was to make French cooking accessible and fun, but Martha Stewart's seemed to keep perfection always visible and always just out of reach. The best chef-writers urge people who like to cook to use their intuition, to experiment, and, most of all, to enjoy both cooking and eating. But with so many choices and so much temptation to excess, the risk is of becoming obsessed with the latest food fad, slaves to fashion. Once again, we ask ourselves, Why do we cook?

Our Best Hope of Happiness

IN 1991, THE MUSEUM OF MODERN ART MOUNTED AN EXHI-
BITION OF PHOTOGRAPHS WITH THE TITLE, *PLEASURES AND*
Terrors of Domestic Comfort. One of the show's most striking photographs, "Mario," by Philip-Lorca Dicorcia, shows a young man in a
dark kitchen, peering into a lighted refrigerator. His expression is sol-
emn, even sad. What is he looking for? Something more, it appears,
than a snack. Mario is alone in the kitchen; in many of the other photographs people stand or sit with others in and around houses, but
they seem detached, looking away from one another. The things in
the houses are those expected of suburban households characteristic
of the fifties, in which perfect American families were supposed to
have dwelt. But the people seem lost, even in familiar surroundings.

Surveying this scene, the radical columnist and poet Katha Pollitt takes note of what seems "all loss, all missed connections." Nevertheless, like the man staring into the refrigerator, she says, "we keep
looking because in the home is the place where, if anywhere, lies our
best hope of happiness."[1] For decade after decade of our twentieth
century the cookbooks have tried to provide the recipe for this happiness. They said it could be achieved through community, family,
science, or technology; through frugality, during the Depression; patriotically, during World War II; easily or with hard work, economically or lavishly. But, in a sense, all the master cooks as authors missed

the point. Method was not the answer; the quest was. For all the risks, this best hope was worth seeking, worth reinventing.

Jody Adams, a Cambridge, Massachusetts, chef well known for her imaginative cooking, first at Michela's restaurant and then at the Rialto, confessed to "a desire to spend time at the table, at home, with company, conversation, and food and drink." She wrote, "I worry about where the family meal is headed in this century. Fewer families gather for a home cooked meal at the end of the day, and if they do, the food is packaged and the TV has a place at the table." A mother of two young children, she emphasized her views by giving a plan for a dinner at her house, "on the table within an hour of the time the groceries were put away."[2]

Her menu is quite different from Martha Stewart's. Pork chops, cabbage, sweet potatoes, and apples, it's a meal that would win the approval of Mrs. Abney. All the ingredients are roasted in the oven, carefully timed to be finished together. The grandeur of her restaurant food is not needed, but there are candles on the table as Jody Adams sits down with her husband and her six-year-old son, the baby in her lap. "It's a lot but it's worth it," she says. "We're a family."[3]

That word "family" is tricky. We know what Adams means when she speaks of hers. Pollitt notes that most of the people in *Pleasures and Terrors of Domestic Comfort* are arranged in groups that would not upset the "family values" folks of the religious right, heterosexual white couples whose children look like them. There is one affecting portrait of a large black man with a tiny child sleeping on his chest, and another of a gay couple sitting on a couch with the mother of one of them. These are only small suggestions of a change in the way we understand the composition of a family.

In 1991 only 25.9 percent of all American households consisted of married couples with children under eighteen, a drop from 40.3 percent in 1970. Twenty-five percent of households consist of people living alone.[4] Nonetheless, the frequently reiterated image of today's family, in which the children eat in front of the television set and the parents grab something to eat when they have time, seems to be inaccurate. A 1990 survey found that "the vast majority (80 percent) of

Americans with children say that on a typical weeknight most of their family eats dinner together." In extended interviews with selected respondents after the poll, people indicated "that despite the pressures on single parents and on families in which both parents work outside the home, families go to great lengths to eat dinner together. Nearly all of these people said eating dinner together provided a peaceful respite from the frenzy of their day. Without it, many said, they would no longer feel as though they were a family." They may open a box of macaroni or eat pizza, or they may follow one of the constant stream of fast recipes produced by newspaper and magazine food writers. Marion Burros of the *New York Times* has succeeded Pierre Franey (who published a collection of recipes from his column, "The Sixty-Minute Gourmet," in 1979) as a leader in the invention of fast, delicious, wholesome dinners. Lillian Gilbreth, the time-and-motion expert of the 1920s, would have admired Burros's efficiency. Burros provides exact step-by-step directions, a game plan, in her terms: when to put the water on to boil and when to cut up the mushrooms, what to purchase already prepared (like chopped onions) to save time. She gives similarly exact dietary information. The menus are often interesting, but this is not creative cooking; there isn't time for that. The twenty-minute dinner, like the half-hour television sitcom, must tell its tale briefly. It makes dinner possible in a life in which everybody is busy. As one woman in the *Times* survey said, "Of course we have dinner together. I was raised that way. That's what families do."[5]

We no longer can accept the Norman Rockwell vision of the American family; we are families with one parent, families of people with no blood relationships, even families of one. Families of many ethnic backgrounds are equally representative. Curiously, a metaphor for this revised understanding of diversity can be found in a new edition of that mid-century American classic, *The Joy of Cooking*.

The first revision in twenty years, this new edition (with a different publisher) appeared in 1997. The title page still lists Irma S. Rombauer as the primary author, but she might have a hard time finding her recipes. Physically the book is much larger than earlier editions:

1100 pages long (my old one is about 850) and a generous inch longer and wider. The book jacket retains the familiar typeface of the title, but behind the bold red *Joy*, shadowy words give away the world of change that has occurred, words like "Asian noodles," "Tapas," "Bean and soy recipes for vegans," "Reduced fat recipes for today's lifestyles." Turning to the table of contents, the reader finds more surprises. The old "Luncheon and Supper Dishes" chapter has vanished. There's a chapter on beans and tofu and another on condiments, marinades, and dry rubs.

The new *Joy* is comprehensive in ways Irma Rombauer never dreamed. It pulls together the trends we've seen since the 1960s. Its international scope is wide. The cuisines of China and Vietnam, of Italy and Ethiopia, and of North Africa and Mexico are represented. Multiethnicity has done wonders for the sandwich section, which used to rely heavily on toast, deviled ham, cheese, and such; now there are recipes for fajitas and burritos, calzone and panini, and roll-ups, along with American diner food like clam rolls and Philadelphia Cheese Steak.

The vegetarian spirit of the seventies is present especially in the chapter called "Beans & Tofu." Many new recipes for dried beans are there, along with instructions for sprouting beans. The mysteries of tofu, tempeh, and seitan are explained.

The standards of restaurant chefs are visible in the elegant Goat Cheese and Walnut Souffles, and perhaps most of all in a new chapter called "Little Dishes," to which no less than sixteen people (many of them chefs) contributed. It finds its raison d'être in a "style of eating [that] became something of a fad in the United States in the 1980s under the name 'grazing.'"[6] This urban restaurant fashion means snacking on an array of interesting small dishes rather than dining in the conventional manner of appetizer, main dish, side dishes, and dessert. While the recipes (several of them are familiar ingredients of catered cocktail parties) certainly can be used individually, the reader is encouraged to replicate this new meal structure at home.

The disappearance of my longtime favorite chapter, "Luncheon and Supper Dishes," points to the one aspect of cooking this *Joy* fails to acknowledge. It offers little advice or encouragement to the cook who wants to make a family meal at the end of a working day with no time to spare. Even the tuna-noodle casserole requires a made-from-scratch cream sauce—the can of mushroom soup that Rombauer considered such a contribution to civilization has disappeared. There is little sense, either, that children are being fed. The suggested menus are few and adult. You can find instructions for cooking a hamburger or a baked potato or for baking brownies in this vast compendium, but you will do so without encouragement. Leftovers, the bane of many an everyday cook, seem not to exist.

In this crowd of chefs who have produced so many tempting recipes and clear explanations of technique, it's hard to find Irma Rombauer. "This book reflects my life," she wrote in the 1943 edition. "It was once merely a private record of what the family wanted, of what friends recommended and of dishes made familiar by foreign travel and given an acceptable Americanization. . . . I have made an attempt to meet the needs of the average household, to make palatable dishes with simple means and to lift everyday cooking out of the commonplace."[7] She knew that kitchens and dining rooms should be common places. She addressed her readers as if she were standing with them at the stove. I miss her personal voice.

————

The tradition that arranging for dinner to happen is a female task is deeply enmeshed in the social fabric. Although the work of the kitchen is becoming less gendered as men reach for the cookbook or at least watch Saturday's numerous cooking shows, a study by the anthropologist Marjorie DeVault in 1991 found that in most households women still bear the responsibility for day-in, day-out feeding. Why do they continue to do it? They say that it's more practical that way, that they are better at it, more experienced, and some admit that they enjoy it.

DeVault concludes that there is something more than pragmatism at work. Behind these superficial reasons, "feeding work in the American family setting is organized, at least in part, through relations of gender inequality." She finds that because the work centers on pleasing others, it "contributes to the culturally produced idea that women and men are different, and that different behaviors are central to 'being' men and women."[8] But we are learning to challenge those rigid categories. Men need not be exclusively masculine, nor women defined by femininity.

As the layers of control are lifted, many people discover the pleasure and satisfaction that were also always there. Zen followers in the 1970s and 1980s articulated a secret many women had always known. Besides the daily repetitive necessities, the coercive commands of the cookbook authors, the mess, fuss, and, sometimes, lack of appreciation, and the hard work, there was something else about cooking. One writer called it "foodmaking as a thoughtful practice."[9] The sensual pleasures and satisfactions of cooking had always been there, but they were, perhaps, better articulated now, in this age when questions of the self and identity were paramount. From the delightful complexities of *The New Basics* to the meditative simplicity of *Tassajara* seems a long way, yet both emphasize respect for ingredients and pleasure in the tasks of preparation.

The women who have stayed with it find pleasure in rattling their pots and pans, developing skills, creating something beautiful and delicious, and feeding people they love. They know the relaxation that comes with kneading bread or stirring soup. They realize they need not resign from the world in favor of cooking. As good subversives, they have made the kitchen a room of their own. If it has sometimes been a trap, it has also been a place to be creative, to have fun, to gather strength for more public work. Men who have crossed the threshold unburdened by the associations of the past have realized these pleasures too.

Women no longer automatically accept that it is their fate to be responsible for dinner (and breakfast and possibly lunch). Many feminists view cooking as a political issue, an insidious means of control. "If women rebel against caring about food," wrote Robin Morgan in February 1980, in the pages of *Ms.* magazine, "it's really a normal reaction to the way this society has confused us with and defined us by food." Society has said it is "natural" for women to feed people, and the language is full of food terms applied to women: "peach," "tomato," "cookie." Women, Morgan said, must understand how the subject has been used against them and construct "a whole new feminist politics of food."[10]

A few years earlier, Morgan, in what she referred to as a "personal retrospective" of the feminist experience, wrote, "They said we [feminists] were 'anti-housewife,' although many of us *were* housewives, and it was not us, but society itself, as structured by men, which had contempt for life-sustenance tasks."[11] The cookbooks that carried social messages about women's lives embedded in their recipes failed in their efforts to attach a recognizably "serious" meaning to cooking. Feminism caused some women to reject cooking but opened the way for understanding the place of cooking as a satisfying activity.

When long-established customs are put in question, people are left to find their own way. Many women have, in cooperation with their families, freed themselves from the sole responsibility for family food. Some families take turns being in charge of food. Many eat out a lot more. Any family member who enjoys cooking may decide to take it on, now that it isn't reserved. The DeVault study showed that women accept doing what they've always done because it seems easier—they know how. Someone who has throughout her entire life been learning and practicing this responsibility may find it hard to stay out of the kitchen while someone else is—perhaps clumsily or slowly—going through the process.

Few women have taken the extreme position of Linda Eyres Delzell who, in the pages of *Ms.* in 1980, wrote, "Three years ago I quit planning and preparing meals." Everybody in her family (two children and a physician husband) fixed his or her own food at his or her own convenience. They ate what they liked and contributed to a grocery list on the refrigerator door. If they ate together, it was just a coincidence. (It is interesting that Delzell continued to do all the grocery shopping.)[12]

In the course of these decades we cooks have done without money (in the Depression), without meat or sugar (in wartime). We have learned clever tricks with canned mushroom soup and the art of making a good Boeuf Bourgignon. We've been scientific and serious with Fannie Farmer and laughed with Julia Child. We've learned about vitamins, minerals, balanced diets, cholesterol, protein. Today, more women participate in more areas of life—and more men cook. The reasons for cooking at all are changing; it has become more a choice, less a necessity. *The Joy of Cooking* still provides a recipe for cherry pie (with four alternative pie crusts) but pie making is no longer a standard by which women are judged.

In a world with a million distractions there are few opportunities to focus on an occupation that involves both mind and body. Whether we choose a ten-minute recipe or an all-day cooking experience, it's possible to find cooking to be an act of renewal rather than depletion, an expression of personality rather than suppression of identity. Creative cooking can be compatible with creative work. Finally we may be able to acknowledge its pleasures without fear of committing ourselves to a daily grind. We do not need to lose our kitchens to keep our freedom.

ONE: MRS. ABNEY'S HAM

1. Richard Hofstadter, *The Age of Reform* (New York: Vintage, 1955), 23.
2. Writers' Program, Work Projects Administration, *Missouri: A Guide to the "Show Me" State* (1941; reprint, New York: Hastings House, 1959), 64, 61.
3. Nina Wilson Badenoch, "Planning the Kitchen," *House & Garden*, November 1922, 76.
4. WPA, *Missouri*, 5–6.
5. *The Napton Memorial Church Cook Book* (Napton, Mo.: n.p., 1928), 17.
6. Ibid., 143.
7. Ibid., 149, 148.
8. Ibid., 27.
9. Ibid., 31, 41.
10. Ibid., 31, 65.
11. Ibid., 35.
12. Ibid., 97, 119, 101.
13. Ibid., 108.
14. Ibid., 122.
15. Mrs. T. J. Kirkpatrick, comp., *The Modern Cook Book* (Springfield, Ohio: Mast, Crowell, & Kirkpatrick, 1890), 188.
16. *Napton Cook Book*, 118.
17. Evelyn G. Halliday and Isabel T. Noble, *Hows and Whys of Cooking* (Chicago: University of Chicago Press, 1946), 62, 60.
18. Mrs. Simon Kander, comp., *The Settlement Cook Book*, 28th ed. (Milwaukee: Settlement Book Co., 1947), 17. Until the late 1940s, manuals like *The*

Settlement Cook Book included instructions for starting and managing wood and coal fires.

19. Ibid., 14–15.

20. *Napton Cook Book*, 23.

21. Christine Frederick, *Household Engineering: Scientific Management in the Home* (Chicago: American School of Home Economics, 1921), 89–90.

22. Kirkpatrick, *Modern Cook Book*, 188.

23. Katherine Jellison, *Entitled to Power: Farm Women and Technology, 1913–1963* (Chapel Hill: University of North Carolina Press, 1993), 55–56.

24. Evelyn Birkby, *Neighboring on the Air: Cooking with the KMA Radio Home-makers* (Iowa City: University of Iowa Press, 1991), 6.

25. *Napton Cook Book*, 134.

TWO: "WE ARE GOING TO LOSE OUR KITCHENS"

1. Dolores Hayden, *The Grand Domestic Revolution: A History of Feminist Designs for American Homes, Neighborhoods, and Cities* (Cambridge: MIT Press, 1981).

2. Melusina Fay Peirce, "Co-operative Housekeeping," part 4, *Atlantic Monthly* 23 (1869): 162.

3. Quoted in "William Dean Howells," *Dictionary of American Biography* (New York: Charles Scribner's Sons, 1932), 5:237.

4. Peirce, "Co-operative Housekeeping," part 1, *Atlantic Monthly* 22 (1868): 522.

5. Alice James, quoted in Kim Townsend, *Manhood at Harvard: William James and Others* (New York: W. W. Norton, 1996), 202.

6. Peirce, "Co-operative Housekeeping," part 2, *Atlantic Monthly* 22 (1868): 682.

7. Ibid., 684.

8. Ibid., 684–85.

9. Peirce, "Co-operative Housekeeping," part 5, *Atlantic Monthly* 23 (1869): 293.

10. Peirce, "Co-operative Housekeeping," part 2, 696.

11. "Record of the Proceedings of the Cambridge Cooperative Housekeeping Society, Beginning with the first meeting, May 1869," unpaged manuscript notebook, Miterachi Papers, Schlesinger Library, Radcliffe College, Cambridge, Mass.

12. Hayden, *Grand Domestic Revolution*, 81–82.

13. Henry Adams, quoted in Townsend, *Manhood at Harvard*, 195.

14. Peirce, "Co-operative Housekeeping," part 3, *Atlantic Monthly* 23 (1869): 29.

15. *Woman's Journal*, quoted in Faye E. Dudden, *Serving Women: Household Service in Nineteenth-Century America* (Middletown: Wesleyan University Press, 1983), 184.

16. *New York Daily Tribune*, quoted in ibid., 185.

17. Lydia Kingsmill Commander, quoted in W. Fitzhugh Brundage, *A Socialist Utopia in the New South: The Ruskin Colonies in Tennessee and Georgia, 1894–1901* (Urbana: University of Illinois Press, 1996), 69.

18. Brundage, *Socialist Utopia*, 6.

19. Ibid., 133.

20. Charlotte Perkins Gilman, *The Home: Its Work and Influence* (1903; reprint, ed. with an introduction by William L. O'Neill, Urbana: University of Illinois Press, 1972), 83.

21. Charlotte Perkins Gilman, "To the Young Wife" [poem], quoted in Polly Wynn Allen, *Building Domestic Liberty: Charlotte Perkins Gilman's Architectural Feminism* (Amherst: University of Massachusetts Press, 1988), 55.

22. Gilman, *The Home*, 113, 127, 132.

23. Hayden, *Grand Domestic Revolution*, 189–95.

24. Charlotte Perkins Gilman, *Women and Economics* (1898; reprint, ed. Carl Degler, New York: Harper and Row, 1966), 267–68.

25. Reva B. Siegel, "Home as Work: The First Woman's Rights Claims concerning Wives' Household Labor, 1850–1880," *Yale Law Journal* 103 (1994): 1073, 1202.

26. Hayden, *Grand Domestic Revolution*, 207.

27. Ibid., 209–10.

28. Brundage, *Socialist Utopia*, 96.

THREE: THE KITCHEN LABORATORY

1. Janet Wilson James, "Ellen Swallow Richards," *Notable American Women, 1607–1950* (Cambridge: Harvard University Press, 1971), 3:146.

2. Margaret Rossiter, *Women Scientists in America: Struggles and Strategies to 1940* (Baltimore: Johns Hopkins University Press, 1982), 65.

3. Fannie Merritt Farmer, *The Boston Cooking-School Cook Book*, rev. ed. (Boston: Little, Brown, 1927), 3–4.

4. Ibid., 357, 347.

5. Ibid., 133.

6. Ibid., 341.

7. Eunice Beecher, *The Law of the Household* (Boston: Small, Maynard, [1912]).

8. Dudden, *Serving Women*, 159.

9. *Electrical Homemaking, with 101 Recipes* (Cleveland: Electrical League of Cleveland, 1926), 25.

10. Ibid., 26.

11. Advertisement, *Time*, July 9, 1928, 31.

12. *Better Homes in Atlanta* (Atlanta, Ga.: n.p., n.d.), unpaged.

13. Ibid.

14. Marie Meloney, "Glorifying the Kitchen," *New York Herald Tribune Magazine*, June 15, 1930, 17.

15. "Test Your Kitchen by Ours," Ibid., 18–19.

16. Blanche Halbert, ed., *The Better Homes Manual* (Chicago: University of Chicago Press, 1931), 475–80.

17. Ibid., 479.

18. "Test Your Kitchen by Ours," 18.

19. Halbert, *Better Homes Manual*, 479.

20. Warren Susman, *Culture as History: The Transformation of American Society in the Twentieth Century* (New York: Pantheon, 1984), 111.

21. Anne Mendelson, *Stand Facing the Stove: The Story of the Women Who Gave America "The Joy of Cooking"* (New York: Henry Holt, 1996), 127.

22. Irma S. Rombauer and Marion Rombauer Becker, *The Joy of Cooking* (Indianapolis: Bobbs-Merrill, 1953), 77.

23. Ibid.

24. Rombauer and Becker, *The Joy of Cooking*, rev. and enl. (Indianapolis: Bobbs-Merrill, 1962), 754, 227.

FOUR: STONE SOUP

1. Warren Susman, *Culture as History: The Transformation of American Society in the Twentieth Century* (New York: Pantheon, 1984), 201.

2. Peter Filene, *Him/Her Self: Sex Roles in Modern America* (New York: Harcourt Brace Jovanovich, 1974), 171.

3. Alice Kessler-Harris, *Women Have Always Worked: A Historical Overview* (Old Westbury, N.Y.: Feminist Press, 1981), 139–40.

4. Quoted in Linda Kerber, "The Obligations of Citizenship," in *U.S. History as Women's History*, ed. Linda K. Kerber, Alice Kessler-Harris, Kathryn Kish Sklar (Chapel Hill: University of North Carolina Press, 1995), 30–31.

5. Ibid.

6. Eleanor Roosevelt, *Eleanor Roosevelt's My Day*, ed. Rochelle Chadakoff, vol. 1 (New York: Pharos, 1989), 69–70. Dated Hyde Park, August 13, 1937.

7. Cora Brown, Rose Brown, and Bob Brown, *Most for Your Money Cookbook* (New York: Modern Age, 1939), 10.

8. Ibid., 9, 22.

9. Ibid., 9–10.

10. Winifred D. Wandersee, *Women's Work and Family Values, 1920–1940* (Cambridge: Harvard University Press, 1981), 107.

11. James Beard, *James Beard's American Cookery* (Boston: Little, Brown, 1972), 90.

12. Kander, *Settlement Cook Book* (1947), 108.

13. Ibid., 109; Rombauer and Becker, *Joy of Cooking* (Indianapolis: Bobbs-Merrill, c. 1964), 181.

14. Irma S. Rombauer, *Streamlined Cooking: New and Delightful Recipes for Canned, Packaged and Frosted Foods and Rapid Recipes for Fresh Foods* (Indianapolis: Bobbs-Merrill, 1939), 42, 44.

15. Rombauer and Becker, *Joy of Cooking* (1975), 178.

16. *Low Cost Food for Health* (Boston: Community Health Association, 1937), 12.

17. Pierre Franey, *Pierre Franey's Kitchen* (New York: Fawcett/Ballantine, 1982), xi.

18. Caroline Bird, *The Invisible Scar* (New York: David McKay, 1966), 275.

19. Brown, Brown, and Brown, *Most for Your Money*, 117.

20. J. C. Furnas, *How America Lives* (London: John Lane, 1943), 175.

21. Dorothy Sterling, letter to the author, September 25, 1991; Brown, Brown, and Brown, *Most for Your Money*, 135–36.

22. Brown, Brown, and Brown, *Most for Your Money*, 4, 72, 70–71.

23. *Low Cost Food for Health*, passim.

24. Brown, Brown, and Brown, *Most for Your Money*, 86.

25. "Summer Meals to Suit Your Pocketbook," *Good Housekeeping*, July 1935, 92–94.

26. Ann Batchelder, "We Suggest," *Ladies' Home Journal*, January 1935, 28.

27. Ida Bailey Allen, *Ida Bailey Allen's Money-Saving Cook Book* (New York: Garden City, 1940), 178.

28. Advertisements, *Good Housekeeping*, June 1930, 118, 183.

29. Mary Lyles Wilson, *Mary Lyles Wilson's New Cook Book*, 6th ed. (Nashville: Southwestern, 1930), 283.

30. Robert Hall, "Foodways in the African Diaspora" (paper delivered at the conference Edible Landscapes, Schlesinger Library, Radcliffe College,

March 27, 1999); Karen Hess, *The Carolina Rice Kitchen* (Columbia: University of South Carolina Press, 1992), 5.

31. Bird, *The Invisible Scar*, 48.

FIVE: THE WAR IN THE KITCHEN

1. Louisa Pryor Skilton, "Victory Lunches: Hearty Food for Sturdy Men," *American Cookery*, March 1943, 348; Harriet H. Hesler, *300 Sugar Saving Recipes* (New York: M. Barrows, 1942), vii.

2. Louise Grant diary, December 9, 27, 1941, January 8, 1942, Strawbery Banke Museum Collection, Portsmouth, N.H.

3. Ibid., December 29, 13, 1941, January 5, February 12, 1942.

4. Ibid., December 19, 24, 31, 1941.

5. John M. Blum, *V Was for Victory: Politics and American Culture during World War II* (New York: Harcourt Brace Jovanovich, 1976), 16.

6. Barbara McLean Ward, "A Fair Share at a Fair Price: Rationing, Resource Management, and Price Controls During World War II," *Produce and Conserve, Share and Play Square: The Grocer and the Consumer on the Home Front Battlefield*, ed. Barbara McLean Ward (Portsmouth, N.H.: Strawbery Banke Museum, 1994), 79–103.

7. Advertisement, *The New Yorker*, September 5, 1942.

8. Harvard Sitkoff, "The American Home Front," in Ward, *Produce and Conserve*, 43.

9. Heller Committee for Research in Social Economics, University of California, *Wartime Budgets* (Berkeley, 1944), 5.

10. Rombauer, *The Joy of Cooking* (Indianapolis: Bobbs-Merrill, 1943), 786.

11. Harry Henderson, "Why the Meat Shortage?" *Woman's Day*, November 1942, 35, 62–63.

12. Grant diary, December 19, 1942.

13. Helen Hokinson, *The New Yorker*, August 22, 1942, 21.

14. Prudence Penny, *Coupon Cooking* (Hollywood, Calif.: Murray and Gee, 1943), 57.

15. A. A. Milne, "The King's Breakfast," in *When We Were Very Young* (New York: Doubleday, 1924), 55.

16. Audre Lorde, "Uses of the Erotic," *Sister Outsider* (Trumansburg, N.Y.: Crossing Press, 1984), quoted in Lisa M. Heldke, "Foodmaking as a Thoughtful Practice," in *Cooking, Eating, Thinking: Transformative Philosophies of Food*, ed. Deane W. Curtin and Lisa M. Heldke (Bloomington: Indiana University Press, 1992), 223.

17. Grant diary, June 28, 1945.

18. Margaret Rudkin, *The Margaret Rudkin Pepperidge Farm Cookbook* (New York: Atheneum, 1963), 64–65, 164.

19. Harvey Levenstein, *Paradox of Plenty: A Social History of Eating in Modern America* (New York: Oxford University Press, 1993), 85.

20. Grant diary, May 29, September 30, October 17, 19, 1942.

21. Roy F. Hendrickson, "If Men Would Only Listen," *Woman's Day*, September 1943, 1.

22. Birkby, *Neighboring on the Air*, 42, 46, 109; advertisement, *American Cookery*, December 1943.

23. Cora Anthony, "Eat Fresh Vegetables," *Woman's Day*, March 1943, 1–3.

24. Rombauer, *Joy of Cooking* (1943), 794.

25. Grant diary, February 1, 13, 1943.

26. Hendrickson, "If Men Would Only Listen," 1.

27. *American Cookery*, Aug.–Sept. 1941, 122.

28. Marjorie Mills, *Cooking on a Ration* (Boston: Houghton Mifflin,1943), 41.

29. Telephone interview with Anna Hamburger, March 1998. Hamburger lived in Wellfleet and taught home economics during the war.

30. Ruth G. Stimson, "Chronology of Events Significant to the Cooperative Extension Service and Its Clients. . . ." Part 4, 1942 and 1943, entry for September 1942 (typescript), Strawbery Banke Museum.

31. Grant diary, October 3, 23, 1943.

32. Students and Faculty of Sarah Lawrence College, Bronxville, N.Y., comps., "Food—a Weapon of Our Nation," in "Nutrition Melodies," 1943 (typescript).

33. Skilton, "Victory Lunches," 348–49.

34. "Nell Giles Packs a Victory Lunch Box for Girls on the Aircraft Assembly Line," *American Cookery*, October 1942, 86–87.

35. Grant diary, December 21, 1944; February 3, January 18, 1945.

36. Ibid., June 23, July 6, 1945.

SIX: TUNA-NOODLE CASSEROLE

1. Arlene Skolnick, *Embattled Paradise: The American Family in an Age of Uncertainty* (New York: Basic Books, 1991), 50.

2. Ibid., 53; Elaine Tyler May, *Homeward Bound: American Families in the Cold War Era* (New York: Basic Books, 1988), 167.

3. *Betty Crocker Picture Cook Book* (New York: McGraw-Hill, c. 1950), 115–16.

4. Ibid., 294, 295.

5. Ludlow Smethurst, letter to the author, January 16, 1995.

6. Skolnick, *Embattled Paradise*, 53.

7. May, *Homeward Bound*, 89.

8. Ibid., 90–91.

9. Poppy Cannon, *The Can-Opener Cookbook* (New York: Thomas Y. Crowell, 1951), 1.

10. Barbara Goodfellow, *Make It Now, Bake It Later* (Arlington, Va.: privately published, 1958), 18.

11. Quoted in Robert Clark, *The Solace of Food: A Life of James Beard* (South Royalton, Vt.: Steerforth, 1996), 160.

12. Robert Sheehan, "Grand Union's Super Supermarkets," *Fortune*, June 1955, 196.

13. Mary Ryan, *Womanhood in America: From Colonial Times to the Present* (New York: Franklin Watts, 1975), 345.

14. Stephanie Coontz, *The Way We Never Were: American Families and the Nostalgia Trap* (New York: Basic Books, 1992), 161.

15. May, *Homeward Bound*, 105.

16. Roald Dahl, "Lamb to the Slaughter," *Someone Like You* (New York: Alfred A. Knopf, 1953), 23–37.

SEVEN: BOEUF BOURGUIGNON AND CHOCOLATE MOUSSE

1. Quoted in Erik Amfitheatrof, *Children of Columbus* (Boston: Little, Brown, 1973), 237.

2. Katherine Kellock, *U.S. One: Maine to Florida* (Federal Writers' Project, 1938), xxvii.

3. Florence Arfmann, comp., *The Time Reader's Book of Recipes* (New York: Dutton, 1949), 213.

4. Barbara Goodfellow, *Make it Now, Bake It Later,* no. 2 (Arlington, Va.: privately published, 1961), 12.

5. "Collectors' Cook Book: Pork," *Woman's Day*, January 1960.

6. "Collectors' Cook Book: Pork; A Treasury of Recipes from Many Lands," *Woman's Day*, February 1966.

7. "Collectors' Cook Book: Frankfurters," *Woman's Day*, July 1966.

8. Mendelson, *Stand Facing the Stove*, 309.

9. June Ball, letter to the author, May 28, 1991.

10. Roberta Ames, *The Complete Electric Skillet-Frypan Cookbook* (New York: Hearthside Press, 1960), passim.

11. "Phineas Beck" [Samuel Chamberlain], "Clémentine in the Kitchen," *Gourmet*, February 1942, 45.

12. *Gourmet*, April 1954, 63.

13. Auxiliary, Easter Seal Rehabilitation Center of Southwestern Connecticut, Inc., comp., *An Uncommon Cook Book* (Stamford, 1978), 57; Friends of the Dover [N.H.] Public Library, *Centennial Cookbook, 1883–1983*, 171.

14. "Collectors' Cook Book: Stews and Ragouts," *Woman's Day*, January 1963.

15. Julia Child, quoted in "Modern Living: Food," *Time*, November 25, 1966, 80.

16. Noel Riley Fitch, *Appetite for Life: The Biography of Julia Child* (New York: Doubleday, 1997), 149–50.

17. Ibid., 197.

18. Julia Child to WGBH, memorandum: "A Series of TV Programs on French Cooking," April 26, 1962, carton 8, folder "WGBH Early Plans, 1962," Julia Child Papers, Schlesinger Library, Radcliffe College, Cambridge, Mass.

19. Recipe from "The French Chef" #126, "To Poach a Chicken," copy distributed by the show, author's files.

20. Julia Child, form letter to reply to this complaint, December 12, 1978, 81-M119, carton 15, Child Papers.

21. Ibid.

22. Veronica Foley to Child, June 3, 1965, carton 1, ibid.

23. Jim Kitchak to Child, n.d. [acknowledged 2/7/80]; Susan Marcum to Child, August 12, 1980, carton 15, ibid.

24. Kenneth J. St. Onge, Riverside, R.I. to Child, November 24, 1964; Susan Rumfield, Chicago, to Child, March 10, 1971, carton 1, ibid.

25. Steven Mintz and Susan Kellogg, *Domestic Revolutions: A Social History of the American Family* (New York: Free Press, 1988), 204.

26. Mrs. Cliff Haslam, Victoria, B. C., to Child, n.d., folder "Fan Mail 1979–1981," 81-M119, carton 15, Child Papers.

27. Mrs. Arthur R. Currey, Pine Bluff, Arkansas, to Child, August 20, 1969, carton 1, ibid.

28. Craig Claiborne, foreword to *The Pleasures of Chinese Cooking*, by Grace Zia Chu (New York: Simon and Schuster, 1962).

29. Mrs. Merle Smith, Jr., to Child, November 28, 1967, carton 1, Child Papers.

1. Regina M. Morantz, "Making Women Modern: Middle Class Women and Health Reform in 19ᵗʰ Century America," *Journal of Social History* 10 (1977): 500.

2. James C. Whorton, *Crusaders for Fitness: the History of American Health Reformers* (Princeton: Princeton University Press, 1982), 300.

3. Gayelord Hauser, *Be Happier, Be Healthier* (New York: Farrar, Straus and Young, 1952), iv; *The Gayelord Hauser Cook Book* (New York: Coward-McCann, 1946), vii–viii, vii.

4. *Time*, December 18, 1972, 72.

5. Adelle Davis, *Let's Cook It Right* (New York: Harcourt Brace, 1947), 5.

6. Davis, *Let's Cook It Right,* rev. ed. (1962), 4–5, 13.

7. Ibid., 7.

8. Adelle Davis, *Let's Eat Right to Keep Fit* (New York: Harcourt Brace Jovanovich, 1954), 19.

9. Coontz, *The Way We Never Were,* 151.

10. Warren Belasco, *Appetite for Change: How the Counterculture Took on the Food Industry, 1966–1988* (New York: Random House, 1989), 72.

11. Frances Moore Lappé, *Diet for a Small Planet,* rev. ed. (New York: Ballantine, 1975), xvii.

12. Ibid., 143.

13. Lappé, *Diet for a Small Planet* (New York: Ballantine, 1971), xiv.

14. Lappé, *Diet* (1975), xviii.

15. Laurel Robertson, Carol Flinders, and Bronwen Godfrey, *Laurel's Kitchen: A Handbook for Vegetarian Cookery and Nutrition* (Berkeley: Nilgiri Press, 1976), 56, 51.

16. Ibid., 62, 68.

17. Ibid., 67.

18. Ibid., 21.

19. Ibid., 29.

20. Bethami Auerbach, "The Search for the Perfect Rye Bread," in *In Her Own Image: Women Working in the Arts,* ed. Elaine Hedges and Ingrid Wendt (Old Westbury, N.Y.: Feminist Press, 1980), 58–60.

21. Edward Espe Brown, *Tassajara Cooking* (San Francisco: Shambhala, 1973), 1, 5.

22. Ibid., 159.

23. Mendelson, *Stand Facing the Stove,* 395.

24. Belasco, *Appetite for Change*, 198–99, 222–23.

25. Pierre Franey, foreword to *Jane Brody's Good Food Book*, by Jane Brody (New York: W. W. Norton, 1985), xx.

26. Brody, *Jane Brody's Good Food Book*, 283.

27. Ibid., 458.

NINE: THE NEW AMERICAN CUISINE AT HOME

1. Alice Waters, *The Chez Panisse Menu Cookbook* (New York: Random House, 1982), xi.

2. Julee Rosso and Sheila Lukins, *The New Basics Cookbook* (New York: Workman, 1989), xiii.

3. Victoria Wise and Susanna Hoffman, *Good and Plenty: America's New Home Cooking* (New York: Harper & Row, 1988), 17–25.

4. Rosso and Lukins, *New Basics*, xii.

5. Martha Stewart, *Martha Stewart's Quick Cook* (1983; reprint, New York: C. N. Potter, 1992), 9.

6. Lorna J. Sass, *Cooking Under Pressure* (New York: Morrow, 1989), 15.

7. David Sarnoff, "The Fabulous Future," *Fortune*, January 1955, 83.

CONCLUSION: OUR BEST HOPE OF HAPPINESS

1. Katha Pollitt, "Pleasures and Terrors of Domestic Comfort," *MOMA Members Quarterly*, Fall 1991, 13.

2. Jody Adams, "Jody at Home," *Rialto News*, Spring 1996, [4].

3. Ibid.

4. "Married With Children: The Waning Icon," *New York Times*, August 23, 1992, Week in Review section, 2.

5. Dena Kleiman, "Even in the Frenzy of the 90's, Dinner Time Is for the Family," *New York Times*, December 5, 1990, 1, C-6.

6. Irma S. Rombauer, *The Joy of Cooking* (Indianapolis: Bobbs-Merrill, 1943), foreword [7].

7. Marjorie Lynn DeVault, "Women and Food: Housework and the Production of Family Life" (Ph.D. diss., Northwestern University, 1984), 233, 234.

8. Heldke, "Foodmaking as a Thoughtful Practice," 216.

9. Robin Morgan, "Why Women Love/Hate Food," *Ms.*, February 1980, 43–44.

10. Robin Morgan, "Rights of Passage," *Ms.*, November 1975, reprinted in *A History of Our Time: Readings on Postwar America*, ed. William H. Chafe and Harvard Sitkoff (New York: Oxford University Press, 1983), 181.

11. Linda Eyres Delzell, "The Family That Eats Together . . . Might Prefer Not To," *Ms.*, February 1980, 56.

Bertholle, Louisette, 120
Better Homes in America, 43–44, 48, 50
Betty Crocker's Picture Cookbook, 91–92
Bird, Caroline, 67
Birk, Dorothy M., 118
biscuits, 155
Bisquick, 93
Black Family Dinner Quilt Cookbook, The, 128
Black Family Reunion Cookbook, The, 128
Blackwell, Alice Stone, 27
body image, 132
Boeuf Bourguinon, 117–19
bomb shelters, 107, 134
Bon Appétit, 149, 152
Bosco, 65
Boston Cooking-School, 35
Boston Cooking-School Cook Book (Farmer), 34–40, 75, 97, 118
box lunches, 85
Bracken, Peg, 99
brand names, 93
bread, 9, 142–44
bread machines, 159
Brody, Jane, 147
Brown, Bob, 55
Brown, Cora, 55
Brown, Edward, 144
Brown, Helen Evans, 103
Brown, Rose, 55
Brown v. Board of Education, 108
Brundage, Fitzhugh, 26
buffet suppers, 100–101, 118
Building of Vital Power, The (Macfadden), 132
Buntin, Mrs., 12

Burke, Billie, 80
Burros, Marion, 164
business model, 28–29, 39
butcher shop, 61
butter, 76, 77, 78, 142, 146

Cabbagetown Café, 140
cake, 12, 99–100, 105
calf hearts, 62
Cambridge Cooperative Housekeeping Society, 22–26
Cambridge Press, 23
Campbell's soups, 57–58
canning groups, 83
canning process, 10, 73–74, 83–84
Cannon, Poppy, 97, 99, 101
can opener, 97, 101
Can-Opener Cookbook, The, 97
capitalism, 32
Carolina Rice Kitchen, The (Hess), 66
Carson, Rachel, 129, 137
cash-and-carry stores, 62
casseroles, 98–102, 111–12, 148
catalogs, 157, 158
chafing dish, 112–13
Chamberlain, Samuel (Phineas Beck), 117
Channing, Grace, 28
Charles and Company, 78
Cheaper by the Dozen, 44
Cheese Whiz, 93, 98
chefs, 149–55
Chef's Catalog, 158
chemical additives, 136
chemistry, 36
Chen, Joyce, 127, 128
Chez Panisse, 150–51
Chez Panisse Menu Cookbook (Waters), 151

nutrition, 42, 64–65, 67, 84; 1990s, 147–48; Graham diet, 130–31; political economy of, 137–38; social messages, 134–35, 148

Oberlin College, 130–31
O'Brien, Honey, 64
Office of Price Administration (OPA), 71, 72, 73, 79, 86
Office of War Information (OWI), 72
Organic Gardening, 137
organic produce, 136, 150
outdoor cooking, 103
Ovaltine, 65, 133
ovens, 12–15, 60, 157, 158–59
Owen, Robert, 31

packaged foods, 92–93, 98–104; cake mixes, 99–100
Paprikas Weiss, 116
patriotism, 43, 50. *See also* World War II
Patterson, Mrs. John C., 13
Peirce, Charles Sanders, 19, 20
Peirce, Melusina Fay (Zina), 19–27, 39, 91
People, 27
Pepperidge Farm bread, 78
physical culture, 131–32
Physical Culture, 131
picnic menu, 151
pie, 64, 92, 168–69
Piggly Wiggly, 47
Pleasures and Terrors of Domestic Comfort, 162, 163
Pleasures of Chinese Cooking, The (Chu), 126–27
Pollitt, Katha, 162, 163

Portsmouth, New Hampshire, 70, 75
presentation of food, 38–39
preserving food, 10, 73–74, 83
pressure cookers, 83, 159–60
Princess Pamela's Soul Food Cookbook, 128
processed foods, 32–33, 42, 47–48, 80–81
produce: local, 150–51, 154; organic, 136, 150; in supermarkets, 113–14, 153–54
professionals, 94–95
progress, 9, 28, 44
progressives, 34, 136
protein, 36, 138–39
psychology of family welfare, 50, 51–52, 54–55, 64
public transportation, 30–31
Pure Food and Drug Act of 1906, 137
pushcarts, 62

Quaker Oats, 146

radios, 15–17, 46, 70, 80, 86
radio shows, 16–17, 64, 80
rationing, 71–72, 74–76, 79, 81–82, 85–86, 89
Red Scare, 31
refrigerators, 41–42, 86
regional foods, 154–55
resistance, 4
respectability, 43–44
restaurants, 56, 140, 149, 150–51, 163
Reynolds, Malvina, 98
Rialto, 163
Richards, Ellen Swallow, 34

Waters, Alice, 150
Web, 160
WGBH television station, 121
whiteness, 3–4
whole grains, 130, 131, 136
Wickersham, George, 53
Williams Sonoma, 158
Wilson, Elizabeth, 61
Windsor, duchess of, 132
Wizard of Oz, The, 80
Woman's Day, 76, 79, 80, 82, 83, 88,
105; casserole recipes, 148;
French recipes, 119–20; hot dog
recipes, 99, 114; pork recipes,
114
Woman's Journal, 25, 27
women: as consumers, 2–3, 42, 46–
47, 88, 97–98; as guardians of
health, 133; as moral guardians,
2, 20, 131, 142; as producers, 9–
11, 17–18, 78, 144; as scientists,
34–35. *See also* gender roles

Women and Economics (Gilman), 27,
34
Women's Alliance, 49, 50
women's movement, 135
Wonder Bread, 9
Woodhull and Claflin's Weekly, 19
working-class women, 30. *See also*
immigrants; servants
Work Projects Administration
(WPA) series, 8–9, 53
World War II: fat saving, 73; meat
rationing, 74–76, 81–82; military imagery for cooking, 69–70,
72, 84–85; preparations, 70–71;
rationing, 71–72, 74–76, 79,
85–86; self-sufficiency, 78
World Wide Web, 160

Young, Jessie, 80

Zen Mountain Center, 144

Mary Drake McFeely was head of the reference department and assistant librarian at Smith College. She has been a resident scholar at the Bellagio Study and Conference Center in Italy, a visiting scholar at the Schlesinger Library, Radcliffe College, and a fellow of the Council on Library Resources. She lives and cooks in Wellfleet and Cambridge, Masachusetts, with her husband, William McFeely.